Oral Sadism and the Vegetarian Personality

Readings From the Journal of Polymorphous Perversity®

Oral Sadism and the Vegetarian Personality

Readings From the Journal of Polymorphous Perversity®

edited by

Glenn C. Ellenbogen, Ph.D.

A STONESONG PRESS BOOK

BRUNNER/MAZEL *Publishers* • New York

Library of Congress Cataloging-in-Publication Data

Oral sadism and the vegetarian personality.

Readings from the Journal of polymorphous perversity.
"A Stonesong Press book."
Includes bibliographies.
1. Psychology—Anecdotes, facetiae, satire, etc.
2. Psychiatry—Anecdotes, facetiae, satire, etc.
I. Ellenbogen, Glenn C.   II. Journal of polymorphous perversity. [DNLM: 1. Psychiatry—humor.   2. Psychology —humor.   WZ 305 063]
PN6231.P785073   1987   150'.207   86–18874
ISBN 0-87630-436-6

Published by
BRUNNER/MAZEL, INC.
19 Union Square
New York, New York 10003

To Ilene—my partner in laughter, love, and play.

Contents

2. Psychoanalysis

3. Psychodiagnostics

4. Psychological Testing

5. Clinical Psychology

6. Educational Psychology and Education

10. Statistics

11. History and Systems of Psychology

12. Psychology Journals

13. Book Reviews

14. Contemporary Issues in Psychology

Collaborative Research and Publication: An Experimental
Investigation of the Dynamics Underlying the Trend

Foreword

"A little nonsense now and then
is relished by the wisest men"

Anonymous

I feel a particular pleasure in being asked to write a foreword to this delightful volume, not only because it allows me to honor it, but also because it gives me an opportunity to retrieve (from the wastebasket) an important early contribution of mine that never saw the light of day.

It was a "modest proposal" for a new approach to psychotherapy, based on the fact that all mammalian neonates, including those of human beings, manifest a prepotent need for mother's milk, or its equivalent. This powerful oral craving persists throughout infancy, and failure to gratify it can, as we know, result in serious physiological and psychological consequences for the developing child.

Proceeding from this base, it seemed reasonable to assume that the reparation of such consequences could be facilitated by employing a richer-than-average form of milk equivalent, such as cream. The working hypothesis for this proposed treatment, therefore, was that if cream were provided, under appropriate circumstances, to neurotic subjects who had suffered severe oral deprivation in their early developmental years, it would provide a corrective therapeutic experience of great value.

The proposed methodology was to be as follows: A properly selected group of such patients would be placed in oversized infant cribs and administered a pint of cream in large nursing bottles three times daily. Supplemental infant food would be added as needed. Significant clinical improvement would be anticipated within three to six months.

Unfortunately, the *Journal of Polymorphous Perversity* had not yet begun publication at the time, and I was unable to obtain an appropriate grant to test my hypothesis. Thus, my chance to have my name forever linked to a unique and original form of psychotherapy was lost. I would have called it—modestly—"Marmor's primal cream therapy."

On a more serious note, many years ago, in 1953, I wrote an article entitled "The Feeling of Superiority: An Occupational Hazard in the Practice of Psychotherapy," in which I was concerned, among other things, about the danger of unconscious arrogance and grandiosity developing in psychotherapists because so much of their daily lives are spent with patients whose transferences lead them to overestimate the wisdom and capacities of their therapists. I added: "[but] it is not only the reactions of his patients that tend to foster 'god-like' feelings in the psychotherapist. The attitude of the lay public is equally significant in this regard. . . . The psychotherapist has become the shaman of our society, the all-seeing father with the Cyclopean eye. He is endowed with god-like perceptiveness . . . he is either Deity or Devil, but rarely is he portrayed as he really is—a person with special training and ability, with human strengths and human frailties."

I know of no better antidote to this occupational hazard than the ability to laugh at one's self, and have the pomposities of jargon in which we tend at times to clothe ourselves—obfuscations that are often mistaken for profundities—deflated. This volume does this superbly—taking on and spoofing, one by one, the pretentious and ponderous pontifications that are often indulged in by various professionals in our field. They are all included here—psychotherapists, psychoanalysts, psychodiagnosticians, psychological testers, clinical psychologists, educational psychologists, industrial psychologists, statisticians, psychohistorians, professional journalists, and book reviewers.

No one who reads the essays in this book will ever again be taken in by the affectations of pedants in our field—and so much the better for all of us! I commend these essays to you with laughter and affection. Read and enjoy!

Judd Marmor, M.D.

Preface

The beginnings of Psychology as a "serious" science can be traced back to Wilhelm Wundt who, in 1879, established the first psychological research laboratory. Almost 100 years later, when I entered graduate school, Psychology had become a *very serious* science—too serious, I thought. I had no way of knowing, then, that I was not alone in thinking as I did. In contrast to all of the serious works that were being written in Psychology, I began writing humorous and satirical articles spoofing Psychology, continuing my writing throughout graduate school and beyond.

In 1980, I founded Wry-Bred Press, a small publishing company devoted to producing and distributing humorous spoofs of Psychology. The first works, which I authored, were humorous "monographs," published under the banner of a fictitious periodical—the *Journal of Polymorphous Perversity.* As these monographs slowly made their way into the hands of psychologists and other mental health professionals over the next few years, I began to receive letters saying, "Your journal is great! Psychologists take themselves and Psychology too seriously. This is just what the field needs. Keep up the good work." In addition, I began to receive submissions "for consideration by your journal." I found more than just a little bit of humor in this situation—receiving humorous pieces for consideration by a journal that did not really exist. Clearly, I was being given the message that there was a real need for a forum whereby psychologists, like myself, could publish humorous and satirical pieces spoofing Psychology.

So, in the summer of 1983, I began to lay the groundwork for a *real* humorous and satirical journal of Psychology, not surprisingly to be called the *Journal of Polymorphous Perversity.* On January 2, 1984, the first issue of the *Journal of Polymorphous Perversity* was released, featuring "Psychotherapy of the Dead" as the lead article.

The articles comprising this anthology were drawn from the first three volumes of the *Journal of Polymorphous Perversity* and from the monograph series. In the three years of its existence, the *Journal of Polymorphous Perversity* has made quite a bit of progress in the difficult task of chipping away at the seriousness of the members of the psychological community. This progress is reflected, for instance, in the fact that more and more state and regional psychological associations have sought permission to reprint the *Journal of Polymorphous Perversity* articles in the official magazines or newsletters of their organizations. But, perhaps one of the most salient examples of the *Journal of Polymorphous Perversity's* impact upon the field rests right in your hands—this anthology, itself, which Brunner/Mazel, Inc., a specialty publisher of *serious* scholarly and professional psychology and psychiatry texts, has chosen to publish! It does, indeed, provide me with hope that the *Journal of Polymorphous Perversity* will continue to make inroads in helping psychologists to be less serious and to take humor more seriously.

New York, New York   Glenn C. Ellenbogen

Acknowledgments

I would like to gratefully acknowledge the help of the following *Journal of Polymorphous Perversity* associate editors, each of whom was kind enough to review the many manuscripts that I forwarded to them for review when the topic touched upon their specialty area:

Milton Spett, Ph.D. (Clinical Psychology), Edward E. Coons, Ph.D. (Comparative/Physiological Psychology), Gregory N. Reising, Ph.D. (Counseling Psychology), Les Halpert, Ph.D. (Developmental Psychology), George E. Rowland, Ph.D. (Engineering Psychology), Richard J. Koppenaal, Ph.D. (Experimental Psychology), James F. Harper, Ph.D. (Forensic Psychology), Robert Perloff, Ph.D. (Industrial/Organizational Psychology), Gordon D. Wolf, Ph.D. (Medical Psychology), Charles F. Levinthal, Ph.D. (Neuropsychology), Christine Holle, M.S.N. (Psychiatric Nursing), Benjamin Strouse, M.S.W. (Psychiatric Social Work), Robert S. Hoffman, M.D. (Psychiatry and Neurology), Estelle Wade, Ph.D. (Psychoanalysis), E. M. Bard, Ph.D. (School Psychology), George Quattrone, Ph.D. (Social Psychology), David O. Herman, Ph.D. (Tests and Measurements).

The decision as to what constitutes "good" humor involves a very subjective process. Thus, the associate editors were rarely in agreement, either among themselves or with me, about which articles merited publication. The responsibility for making the final selections for inclusion in both the regular journal issues and this anthology was ultimately mine and mine alone. The presence of any given article in this anthology should not be construed as reflecting the endorsement of the associate editors.

I would like to thank Dr. Martin Obler, who encouraged me in the development of my humorous perspective on life.

Lastly, I would like to thank the many authors whose works appear in this anthology.

Oral Sadism
and the Vegetarian
Personality

Readings From the Journal of Polymorphous Perversity®

1
Psychotherapy

The Etiology and Treatment of Childhood[1,2]

Jordan W. Smoller

University of Pennsylvania

Childhood is a syndrome which has only recently begun to receive serious attention from clinicians. The syndrome itself, however, is not at all recent. As early as the 8th century, the Persian historian Kidnom made reference to "short, noisy creatures," who may well have been what we now call "children." The treatment of children, however, was unknown until this century, when so-called "child psychologists" and "child psychiatrists" became common. Despite this history of clinical neglect, it has been estimated that well over half of all Americans alive today have experienced childhood directly (Suess, 1983). In fact, the actual numbers are probably much higher, since these data are based on self-reports which may be subject to social desirability biases and retrospective distortion.

The growing acceptance of childhood as a distinct phenomenon is reflected in the proposed inclusion of the syndrome in the upcoming *Diagnostic and Statistical Manual of Mental Disorders, 4th Edition,* or *DSM-IV,* of the American Psychiatric Association (1985). Clinicians are still in disagreement about the significant clinical features of childhood, but the proposed *DSM-IV* will almost certainly include the following core features:

1. Congenital onset
2. Dwarfism
3. Emotional lability and immaturity
4. Knowledge deficits
5. Legume anorexia

---

[1] The author would like to thank all the little people.
[2] This research was funded in part by a grant from Bazooka Gum.

Clinical Features of Childhood

Although the focus of this paper is on the efficacy of conventional treatment of childhood, the five clinical markers mentioned above merit further discussion for those unfamiliar with this patient population.

Congenital Onset

In one of the few existing literature reviews on childhood, Temple-Black (1982) has noted that childhood is almost always present at birth, although it may go undetected for years or even remain subclinical indefinitely. This observation has led some investigators to speculate on a biological contribution to childhood. As one psychologist has put it, "we may soon be in a position to distinguish organic childhood from functional childhood" (Rogers, 1979).

Dwarfism

This is certainly the most familiar clinical marker of childhood. It is widely known that children are physically short relative to the population at large. Indeed, common clinical wisdom suggests that the treatment of the so-called "small child" (or "tot") is particularly difficult. These children are known to exhibit infantile behavior and display a startling lack of insight (Tom & Jerry, 1967).

Emotional Lability and Immaturity

This aspect of childhood is often the only basis for a clinician's diagnosis. As a result, many otherwise normal adults are misdiagnosed as children and must suffer the unnecessary social stigma of being labeled a "child" by professionals and friends alike.

Knowledge Deficits

While many children have IQ's within or even above the norm, almost all will manifest knowledge deficits. Anyone who has known a real child has experienced the frustration of trying to discuss any topic that requires some general knowledge. Children seem to have little knowledge about the world they live in. Politics, art, and science—children are largely ignorant of these. Perhaps it is because of this ignorance, but the sad fact is that most children have few friends who are not, themselves, children.

Legume Anorexia

This last identifying feature is perhaps the most unexpected. Folk wisdom is supported by empirical observation—children will rarely eat their vegetables (see Popeye, 1957, for review).

Causes of Childhood

Now that we know what it is, what can we say about the causes of childhood? Recent years have seen a flurry of theory and speculation from a number of perspectives. Some of the most prominent are reviewed below.

Sociological Model

Emile Durkind was perhaps the first to speculate about sociological causes of childhood. He points out two key observations about children: 1) the vast majority of children are unemployed, and 2) children represent one of the least educated segments of our society. In fact, it has been estimated that less than 20% of children have had more than a fourth grade education.

Clearly, children are an "out-group." Because of their intellectual handicap, children are even denied the right to vote. From the sociologist's perspective, treatment should be aimed at helping assimilate children into mainstream society. Unfortunately, some victims are so incapacitated by their childhood that they are simply not competent to work. One promising rehabilitation program (Spanky & Alfalfa, 1978) has trained victims of severe childhood to sell lemonade.

Biological Model

The observation that childhood is usually present from birth has led some to speculate on a biological contribution. An early investigation by Flintstone and Jetson (1939) indicated that childhood runs in families. Their survey of over 8,000 American families revealed that over half contained more than one child. Further investigation revealed that even most non-child family members had experienced childhood at some point. Cross-cultural studies (e.g., Mowgli & Din, 1950) indicate that familial childhood is even more prevalent in the Far East. For example, in Indian and Chinese families, as many as three out of four family members may have childhood.

Impressive evidence of a genetic component of childhood comes from a large-scale twin study by Brady and Partridge (1972). These authors studied over 106 pairs of twins, looking at concordance rates for childhood. Among identical or monozygotic twins, concordance was unusually high (.92), i.e., when one twin was diagnosed with childhood, the other twin was almost always a child as well.

Psychological Models

A considerable number of psychologically-based theories of the development of childhood exist. They are too numerous to review here. Among the more familiar models are Seligman's "learned childishness" model. According to this model, individuals who are treated like children eventually give up and become children. As a counterpoint to such theories, some experts have claimed that childhood does not really exist. Szasz (1980) has called "childhood" an expedient label. In seeking conformity, we handicap those whom we find unruly or too short to deal with by labeling them "children."

Treatment of Childhood

Efforts to treat childhood are as old as the syndrome itself. Only in modern times, however, have humane and systematic treatment protocols been applied. In part, this increased attention to the problem may be due to the sheer number of individuals suffering from childhood. Government statistics (DHHS) reveal that there are more children alive today than at any time in our history. To paraphrase P.T. Barnum: "There's a child born every minute."

The overwhelming number of children has made government intervention inevitable. The nineteenth century saw the institution of what remains the largest single program for the treatment of childhood—so-called "public schools." Under this colossal program, individuals are placed into treatment groups based on the severity of their condition. For example, those most severely afflicted may be placed in a "kindergarten" program. Patients at this level are typically short, unruly, emotionally immature, and intellectually deficient. Given this type of individual, therapy is of necessity very basic. The strategy is essentially one of patient management and of helping the child master basic skills (e.g., finger-painting).

Unfortunately, the "school" system has been largely ineffective. Not only is the program a massive tax burden, but it has failed even to slow down the rising incidence of childhood.

Faced with this failure and the growing epidemic of childhood, mental health professionals are devoting increasing attention to the treatment of childhood. Given a theoretical framework by Freud's landmark treatises on childhood, child psychiatrists and psychologists claimed great successes in their clinical interventions.

By the 1950s, however, the clinicians' optimism had waned. Even after years of costly analysis, many victims remained children. The following case (taken from Gumbie & Pokey, 1957) is typical.

> Billy J., age 8, was brought to treatment by his parents. Billy's affliction was painfully obvious. He stood only 4'3" high and weighed a scant 70 pounds, despite the fact that he ate voraciously. Billy presented a variety of troubling symptoms. His voice was noticeably high for a man. He displayed legume anorexia and, according to his parents, often refused to bathe. His intellectual functioning was also below normal—he had little general knowledge and could barely write a structured sentence. Social skills were also deficient. He often spoke inappropriately and exhibited "whining behavior." His sexual experience was non-existent. Indeed, Billy considered women "icky."
>
> His parents reported that his condition had been present from birth, improving gradually after he was placed in a school at age 5. The diagnosis was "primary childhood." After years of painstaking treatment, Billy improved gradually. At age 11, his height and weight have increased, his social skills are broader, and he is now functional enough to hold down a "paper route."

After years of this kind of frustration, startling new evidence has come to light which suggests that the prognosis in cases of childhood may not be all gloom. A critical review by Fudd (1972) noted that studies of the childhood syndrome tend to lack careful follow-up. Acting on this observation, Moe, Larrie, and Kirly (1974) began a large-scale longitudinal study. These investigators studied two groups. The first group comprised 34 children currently engaged in a long-term conventional treatment program. The second was a group of 42 children receiving no treatment. All subjects had been diagnosed as children at least 4 years previously, with a mean duration of childhood of 6.4 years.

At the end of one year, the results confirmed the clinical wisdom that childhood is a refractory disorder—virtually all symptoms persisted and the treatment group was only slightly better off than the controls.

The results, however, of a careful 10-year follow-up were startling. The investigators (Moe, Larrie, Kirly, & Shemp, 1984) assessed the original cohort on a variety of measures. General knowledge and emotional maturity were assessed with standard measures. Height was assessed by the "metric system" (see Ruler, 1923), and legume appetite by the Vegetable Appetite Test (VAT) designed by Popeye (1968). Moe et al. found that subjects improved uniformly on all measures. Indeed, in most cases, the subjects appeared to be symptom-free. Moe et al. report a spontaneous remission rate of 95%, a finding which is certain to revolutionize the clinical approach to childhood.

These recent results suggest that the prognosis for victims of childhood may not be so bad as we have feared. We must not, however, become too complacent. Despite its apparently high spontaneous remission rate, childhood remains one of the most serious and rapidly growing disorders facing mental health professionals today. And, beyond the psychological pain it brings, childhood has recently been linked to a number of physical disorders. Twenty years ago, Howdi, Doodi, and Beauzeau (1965) demonstrated a six-fold increased risk of chicken pox, measles, and mumps among children as compared with normal controls. Later, Barby and Kenn (1971) linked childhood to an elevated risk of accidents—compared with normal adults, victims of childhood were much more likely to scrape their knees, lose their teeth, and fall off their bikes.

Clearly, much more research is needed before we can give any real hope to the millions of victims wracked by this insidious disorder.

References

American Psychiatric Association (1985). *The diagnostic and statistical manual of mental disorders, 4th edition: A preliminary report.* Washington, D.C.: APA.

Barby, B., & Kenn, K. (1971). The plasticity of behavior. In B. Barby & K. Kenn (Eds.), *Psychotherapies R Us.* Detroit: Ronco Press.

Brady, C., & Partridge, S. (1972). My dad's bigger than your dad. *Acta Eur. Age, 9,* 123–126.

Flintstone, F., & Jetson, G. (1939). Cognitive mediation of labor disputes. *Industrial Psychology Today, 2,* 23–35.

Fudd, E. J. (1972). Locus of control and shoe-size. *Journal of Footwear Psychology, 78,* 345–356.

Gumbie, G., & Pokey, P. (1957). A cognitive theory of iron smelting. *Journal of Abnormal Metallurgy, 45,* 235–239.

Howdi, C., Doodi, C., & Beauzeau, C. (1965). Western civilization: A review of the literature. *Reader's Digest, 60,* 23–25.

Moe, R., Larrie, T., & Kirly, Q. (1974). State childhood vs. trait childhood. *TV Guide,* May 12–19, 1–3.

Moe, R., Larrie, T., Kirly, Q., & Shemp, C. (1984). Spontaneous remission of childhood. In W. C. Fields (Ed.), *New hope for children and animals.* Hollywood: Acme Press.

Popeye, T. S. M. (1957). The use of spinach in extreme circumstances. *Journal of Vegetable Science, 58,* 530–538.

Popeye, T. S. M. (1968). Spinach: A phenomenological perspective. *Existential Botany, 35,* 908–913.

Rogers, F. (1979). *Becoming my neighbor.* New York: Soft Press.

Ruler, Y. (1923). Assessing measurement protocols by the multi-method multiple regression index for the psychometric analysis of factorial interaction. *Annals of Boredom, 67,* 1190–1260.

Spanky, D. & Alfalfa, Q. (1978). Coping with puberty. *Sears Catalogue,* 45–46.

Suess, D. R. (1983). A psychometric analysis of green eggs with and without ham. *Journal of Clinical Cuisine, 245,* 567–578.

Temple-Black, S. (1982). Childhood: An ever-so sad disorder. *Journal of Precocity, 3,* 129–134.

Tom, C., & Jerry, M. (1967). Human behavior as a model for understanding the rat. In M. de Sade (Ed.), *The rewards of punishment.* Paris: Bench Press.

Further Readings

Christ, J. H. (1980). Grandiosity in children. *Journal of Applied Theology, 1,* 1–1000.

Joe, G. I. (1965). Aggressive fantasy as wish fulfillment. *Archives of General MacArthur, 5,* 23–45.

Leary, T. (1969). Pharmacotherapy for childhood. *Annals of Astrological Science, 67,* 456–459.

Kissoff, K. G. B. (1975). Extinction of learned behavior. Paper presented to the Siberian Psychological Association, 38th Annual Meeting, Kamchatka.

Smythe, C., & Barnes, T. (1979). Behavior therapy prevents tooth decay. *Journal of Behavioral Orthodontics, 5,* 79–89.

Potash, S., & Hoser, B. (1980). A failure to replicate the results of Smythe and Barnes. *Journal of Dental Psychiatry, 34,* 678–680.

Smythe, C., & Barnes, T. (1980). Your study was poorly done: A reply to Potash and Hoser. *Annual Review of Aquatic Psychiatry, 10,* 123–156.

Potash, S., & Hoser, B. (1981). Your mother wears army boots: A further reply to Smythe and Barnes. *Archives of Invective Research, 56,* 570–578.

Smythe, C., & Barnes, T. (1982). Embarrassing moments in the sex lives of Potash and Hoser: A further reply. *National Enquirer,* May 16.

Psychotherapy of the Dead

Samuel E. Menahem, Ph.D.

It is time to "bury the myth" that certain people are untreatable by modern psychotherapy. In recent years people with untreatable "narcissistic character disorders" have suddenly become treatable. It is the contention of this author that there is one group that has been totally neglected by psychotherapists—the dead. Why have they been so ignored? Probably because fat cat therapists only want to take on articulate, motivated patients. Well, it's time for these lazy doctors to get off their dimpled derrieres and "break new ground." People who are dying to get into treatment can no longer be ignored. The author is now treating dead patients and training young therapists to do the same.

Review of the Literature

An exhaustive review of the psychological literature turned up only one article related to the subject of therapy of the dead. Dr. I. M. Bananas (1916) reported that death was the crucial turning point in his treatment of Frau Rigormortis, an arrogant, vindictive patient. Dr. Bananas did a five-year follow-up with the patient's family. They reported that there were no incidents of arrogant behavior since the patient's death. Thus, the case was considered a complete cure.

Dead Silence

Many beginning psychotherapists have trouble with long silences during the therapeutic hour. The author has found that one of the best ways to desensitize psychologists in training is to assign them a dead patient. Techniques to deal with the silence include:

1. *Intermittent questioning of the corpse*, e.g., "What brings you here today?," "What would you really like to get out of therapy?," and "If you were a tree, what kind of tree would you be?"

2. *The Gestalt hot seat technique:* The cadaver is placed on a chair facing the therapist and encouraged to report "exactly what he is feeling *right now.*"

3. *Tentative interpretations,* e.g., "You seem to be expressing hostility toward me which you would rather direct at your mother" and "There seems to be a marked passive-aggressive trend in your silence."

4. *Rational-Emotive therapy:* The therapist attempts through logical reasoning to convince the patient that he is nothing more than a whining baby who thinks he can push people around simply because he's dead. An example of a patient's faulty logic and the therapist's analysis follows. (Communication was established through medium Madame Mediocre.)

   A. Nobody ever liked me when I was alive.
   B. I am now dead.
   C. Nobody will ever like me.

The rational-emotive therapist proceeded to argue that "even if nobody ever liked you, there is no reason to weep and wail and gnash your teeth telepathically. So what if people didn't like you— who gives a shit! Stop that irrational other worldly whining and do something to help yourself. Get a ghost writer, learn the cha cha, do something!"

Transference

Part of the beauty of working with the dead patient is the total lack of transference problems. There is literally nothing to be "worked through." It was noted, however, that when a dead patient was placed in water, a "floating transference" developed immediately. Many of the psychoanalytic therapists were very patient in waiting for either a positive or a negative transference to develop. These therapists believe that cure could be effected only through the development and working through of this "transference neurosis." These therapists spent hundreds of hours carefully observing the affect of the patient. All therapists noticed a certain stiffness and "flattening of affect" as the sessions continued over several months. Many of the therapists also reported a pungent odor, possibly indicative of sweating (anxiety) or passing flatus (passive-aggressive phenomenon). Many therapists also reported a marked indifference of their dead patients, even when the most provocative statements were made, e.g., "Your mother wears combat boots," or "Your father was a leprechaun." This indifference was hypothesized to be related to erotic longings for passive union with an omnipotent figure.

Countertransference

It has long been accepted that therapeutic impasses can be broken through by the therapist observing his own countertransferential feelings and then using them in the context of psychotherapy. The following exchange was typical of the use of this principle in the psychotherapy of the late I. M. Boring of Beaver Falls, Pennsylvania. The therapist was Marci Cystic, Ph.D.

Dr. C.:   How are you feeling today?
Mr. B.:   (Silence—5 minutes pass.)
Dr. C.:   You seem very quiet.
Mr. B.:   (Silence—10 minutes pass.)
Dr. C.:   Your silence is driving me crackers!
Mr. B.:   (Silence—5 minutes pass.)
Dr. C.:   (Angrily) Say something! Anything!
Mr. B.:   (Silence—20 minutes pass.)
Dr. C.:   (Shaking the patient) You're not getting any better. I've tried everything! What do you want? You want me to beg? All right. (Gets down on all fours and imitates a dog begging.) Arf! Arf!
Mr. B.:   (Silence—5 minutes pass.)
Dr. C.:   (Sobbing) Get out of my office you bag of bones you!
Mr. B.:   (Doesn't move)
Dr. C.:   (Sobbing uncontrollably) If only you knew how much I want you to get better. . . . You'd behave differently . . . I know it.

Dr. Cystic analyzed the countertransference with her analyst, Dr. Om Nicient. The following is an excerpt from that session.

Dr. N.:   So how is that difficult patient of yours?
Dr. C.:   Which one?
Dr. N.:   The Dead Head.
Dr. C.:   Oy Mein Gott! Do we have to discuss him?
Dr. N.:   Is it painful?

Dr. C.:   Is duck greasy?

Dr. N.:   Not if you cook it right!

Dr. C.:   I guess I'm ducking the issue.

Dr. N.:   Flight of ideas?

Dr. C.:   No, I'm chickening out . . . I got to face the music. I'm not helping Mr. Boring.

Dr. N.:   And how do you feel as he sits there in silence?

Dr. C.:   Helpless . . . (sobbing) . . . like a lost little girl. . . . And when I feel helpless I get angry.

Dr. N.:   He won't do what you want and get better?

Dr. C.:   That's it! He won't respond. No matter what I do or say. He just sits there!!

Dr. N.:   And you want to get a rise out of him?

Dr. C.:   Yes! And he won't respond.

Dr. N.:   Does this situation remind you in any way of you and your mother?

Dr. C.:   Yes! She never came (crying hysterically) when I cried . . . I called and called and I couldn't make her come to me. I couldn't make her do what I wanted.

Thus we see the rich material elicited by analyzing the countertransference. The dead patient didn't move but the therapist did. She moved to Purdue, Indiana and opened a Chicken D Light franchise.

Special Problems—Reluctance to Pay Bills

One hundred percent of all dead patients showed a marked reluctance to pay their bills. These dead beats think that just because they're deceased they can get away with murder. Thus, it must be emphasized at the first session (preferably held when the patient is still alive) that payment must be made well in advance. Then, someone in the estate must be appointed to pay the bill monthly. Freud (1931) mentioned this problem briefly in his classical paper "Analysis terminable or interminable." He stated "many analyses are truly interminable due to the depth of unconscious bulemia. . . . Thus, the analyst must make some arrangement to continue the analysis and *payment* (italics ours) interminably." It is rumored that Freud's heirs are still collecting fees from the estate of a rich American, D. Warbucks, whose interminable analysis centered on the idea that he was a cartoon character.

Death Is Not an Ending, It's a Beginning

This article is not intended to be the last word on psychotherapy of the dead. It was intended to stimulate the stagnant professionals who are reluctant to treat difficult people. The public must become aware of the neglect of the mental health of the dead. Only a public outcry will make services available in the fertile field of the dead. More research is necessary so that better techniques can be added to the therapeutic armamentarium.

Psychotherapy of the Dead Revisited: Biological Approaches to the Treatment of a Difficult Patient Population

Terrel L. Templeman, Ph.D.

A recent article by Menahem (1984) would leave members of the psychological community with the impression that psychotherapy is the *only* treatment of the dead. This, however, is hardly the case. Biological approaches to treating this serious deteriorated state are generally considered by members of the medical community to be the treatment of choice (Choice, 1984).

The work of Frankenstein and others in Germany in the last century first showed that ECT is quite effective in stimulating previously inert patients. Electrical stimulation has proven particularly effective in eliminating waxy flexibility and unresponsiveness so characteristic of these individuals. The animal literature has replicated these findings as well (Galvani, 1780). Curiously, intracranial stimulation studies with dead rats have shown these animals to self-stimulate at much lower rates than live controls, suggesting that neurochemical reward pathways in dead brains are depleted of particular neurotransmitters.

These results have led to numerous clinical trials of psychotropic agents with the dead. Generally, psychomotor stimulants, such as amphetamines and antidepressants, produce some lifting of mood in the dead, without significant changes in activity levels. Neuroleptics have been shown to successfully diminish agitation and delusional behavior, often resulting in the dead becoming much more manageable in psychotherapy. Lithium treatment has also been shown to preserve a number of lifelike qualities in dead persons, especially when bathed in the salt solution. The success of this rather unique application of lithium may be related to the notorious noncompliance of dead persons in sticking to any medication regime. Fortunately, external application or injectable forms of medications are available.

18

Biological approaches to this condition are based upon the firm belief that death has a strong genetic component. Research by the author and his colleagues at the Oregon Trail of Technology strongly support this assumption. The authors have studied probands of dead patients for the past 40 years and have found that first-order relatives of dead persons are themselves dead within 10 to 40 years after the death of the target person. The authors are currently attempting to replicate these findings with dead monozygotic twins.

In summary, although psychotherapy certainly has some usefulness in treating the dead, the author here strongly suggests that psychotherapy be used only as an adjunct to biological approaches that have been proven safe and effective, although a bit messy.

References

Choice, M.C. (1984). My favorite treatments. *Medicus Actingupica, 211,* 1135–1203.

Galvani, L. (1780). Why the frog twitched. *Scientific Italian, 47,* 31–42.

Menahem, S.E. (1984). Psychotherapy of the dead. *Journal of Polymorphous Perversity, 1*(1), 3–6.

Developing Insight in Intensive-Extensive Psychodynamic Psychotherapy: A Case Study

Don Yutzler, Ph.D.

Although a voluminous, if not tedious, literature exists on the theoretical construct of insight and its conceptual and dynamic underpinnings, as well as its cognitive and affective precursors and concomitants, little in the way of hard clinical data, drawn from actual real-life therapy cases, has been cited as a means of illustrating the dynamics of insight and "the working through process." The author presents, here, an annotated transcript of therapy sessions with one of his more successful therapy patients in order to vividly illustrate the development of therapeutic insight.

This is the case of a 34-year-old Caucasian male, who sought psychodynamic psychotherapy in order to gain insight into why he had left his ex-wife several years earlier. After a great deal of self-exploration, as well as another marriage and two children, the patient now wanted to embark on a formal journey of self-understanding.

The treatment began with 8 sessions of therapy, during which rapport and a strong "working alliance" were established. The following crucial interchange occurs in the 9th session:

Therapist: So, tell me about your ex-wife.
Patient: She was a short woman.

As is evident, this purely descriptive reply reflects no true insight. Note also the therapist's technique which, although highly directive, remains remarkably free of any countertransferential cathexes.

By the 14th visit, the therapist assessed that the patient was ready to tolerate more intensive, affectively charged material and so begins to probe more daringly:

Therapist: So, tell me about your ex-wife.
Patient: As I told you, she was a short woman.

20

Therapist: Um-hmm. Tell me more.
Patient: Well, she weighed about 180 pounds.

In this lively interchange, we immediately note the gains in self-understanding. Although to the naive observer this patient seems rather superficial, the therapist begins to speculate that perhaps the patient is only superficial on the surface.

Again, to the casual listener, the juxtaposition of these descriptive concepts could immediately bring to mind an interpretative intervention, i.e., the woman was obese. But this patient clearly is not yet ready to draw such a conclusion himself and it would be a serious error if the therapist were to precipitously and wantonly blurt out such an anatomical observation. A premature insight could be extremely detrimental to the course of therapy, perhaps shortening it a great deal, perhaps even rendering any further sessions altogether unnecessary. Wisely, the therapist waits.

The next stage of therapy is focused on strengthening the patient's defenses to prepare him to handle the truth. Although the therapist thinks the patient is ready, he has erred, as the following dialogue in the 26th meeting reveals:

Therapist: 12 sessions ago, you described your ex-wife as a short
               woman weighing 180 pounds. Have you given any further
               thought to these two ideas?
Patient: No.
Therapist: Why not?
Patient: I don't know.
Therapist: Would you like to know?
Patient: I don't know. Do you think it's important?
Therapist: Important? I didn't say it was important. Do you think
               it is?
Patient: I asked you first.

Here, it is evident that the therapist has pushed too hard, and the patient is decompensating. The patient shows this by missing the next 2 appointments, thus requiring 4 more to explore resistance and billing issues.

A breakthrough occurs in the 33rd session when the patient refers to his ex-wife as a "tubster." The therapist, unfamiliar with this slang expression, asks for clarification:

Therapist: What?
Patient: Tubster.
Therapist: No, I mean what do you mean?
Patient: She was fat.

Here, the patient is obviously in touch with deeper levels of emotion, for he could have chosen a less pejorative term, e.g. "pleasingly plump," "rotund," or "the wide ride." In "fat," we have hit a nerve. But it was still too early to press for further insight. What remained, of course, was a fuller understanding of the many rolls of the ex-wife's fat in their marriage and its demise.

Finally, in the 40th session, the patient arrives at a marvelous insight:

Therapist: So, why did you leave your wife?
Patient: I just couldn't stand that short, stupid, fat woman any longer!

So this was it. He had left her because she lacked height and depth, while being overly wide. Notice the exclamation point at the end of the patient's statement, clearly signifying his angry yet liberated tone. Here, we have full simultaneous cognitive and affective insight.

The author is pleased to report that the treatment was successfully concluded in only 12 more sessions, as termination issues were worked through to satisfy the therapist's needs for closure and further income to cover malpractice insurance.

The Effective Ingredient in Psychotherapy: An Alternative to the Spontaneous Remission Hypothesis

Ann V. Deaton, Ph.D.
The Brown Schools

Mary Ellen Olbrisch, Ph.D.
University of Texas at Austin

Evidence from several sources is presented to support the hypothesis that it is the therapist's lack of involvement with the patient that is the critical ingredient in psychotherapy. This evidence would suggest that typical control groups used in psychotherapy research may be inappropriate, since patients in these groups actually receive the strongest "dose" of the effective ingredient. A more modest interactional hypothesis is also presented, and implications for research and practice are discussed.

Since Eysenck's challenge to psychotherapy researchers in 1952, there has been ongoing debate about whether or not psychotherapy can be conclusively demonstrated to be effective. Despite intense efforts by the profession of psychology to prove once and for all the efficacy of psychotherapeutic interventions in treating mental and emotional problems, the research findings thus far have remained equivocal, with failures to find significant effects variously attributed to deterioration effects (Lambert, Bergin, & Collins, 1977), the failure to implement treatments in their strongest form (Sechrest, West, Phillips, Redner, & Yeaton, 1979), the ethical and methodological problem in creating a true "no treatment" control group, and the spontaneous remission which occurs even without treatment (Rachman, 1971).

Among the issues facing researchers and therapists alike is the basic question: "What is psychotherapy?" More important, what are its effective components? Numerous ingredients have been proposed as essential in the recipe for psychotherapy. These include such things as the installation of hope, the existence of an empathic, warm, and genuine relationship, support, catharsis, and the uncovering of unconscious conflicts. It is the purpose of this article to speculate anew on: (a) what the crucial element in psychotherapy might be; and (b) how, on the basis of a model of psychotherapy using this central defining feature, much of the confusion about equivocal and negative results thus far can be explained away.

In the effort to define what is and is not psychotherapy, one question that often arises is that of how a therapeutic relationship differs from a friendship. If we were to choose a random sample of clients and ask them why they chose to discuss their problems with a therapist rather than a friend, many would say that they felt a therapist could be objective whereas a friend could not. Thus, it seems that to a number of people the aspect of psychotherapy which is most crucial, at least on some level, is a lack of personal involvement with the therapist.

Background

There are a number of indications in the literature and techniques of therapy that suggest a widespread belief that therapist distance from or lack of involvement with a client is, indeed, one of the most essential and effective components of psychotherapy. Freud's psychoanalytic technique indicated his realization of this aspect when he refrained from becoming involved with his clients by sitting outside of their field of vision and saying as little as possible during a session. Behavior therapists have also become convinced of the validity of this position as they have turned increasingly to the most effective techniques of self-monitoring and self-reward and away from the extrinsically motivating methods which require therapist intervention. Recent studies (Garfield, 1978) indicating that the average number of sessions for a patient is minimal (approximately 6) seem to further suggest that lack of extended involvement is effective.

At the other extreme of this lack of involvement between client and therapist is the extreme involvement represented by sexual intimacy in the therapeutic relationship. Recent discussion of sexual intimacy and its potentially harmful effects upon clients indicate that the profession and public as a whole place a great deal of emphasis on the importance of distance in a therapeutic relationship if psychotherapy is to be effective.

Support for This Model

To test out the assumption of lack of involvement as the effective component of psychotherapy, one must look at the literature of the efficacy of psychotherapy. If, in fact, lack of involvement is crucial, then one would expect that the less involved with a therapist, the more a client should improve. Thus, a client should accomplish most in the first few sessions of therapy and with a therapist with whom he or she has had no prior contact.

Some of the most interesting research on the effectiveness of psychotherapy has been done in recent years, as the advent of national health insurance has made it an economic issue. In an analysis of the most cost-effective means of including therapy as a health service benefit, Follette and Cummings (1967) found that patients with only one session reduced dramatically their utilization of medical services. These results are certainly in keeping with the model presented here, i.e., even with minimal involvement with a therapist, patients improved. In addition, Cummings and Follette (1976) conducted an eight-year follow-up of 85 of these clients which revealed that only two could recall their therapist's name—certainly an indication of their lack of involvement with the therapist. More recently, Cummings (1977) reported that, by reducing the number of therapy sessions from two or three times per week to once a month or once every other month, dramatic improvements were made.

Another well-known finding which is readily explained by this model is that of Eysenck's (1952) initial analysis of psychotherapy's effectiveness, where he presented evidence that control groups improve as much as treatment groups. In fact, according to Eysenck, there was an inverse relationship between amount of therapy received and percentage of patients who improved with that type of therapy. This is a still stronger indication of the importance of staying uninvolved and maintaining distance.

Although hardly meant to be an exhaustive examination of the literature, the examples above clearly show how lack of involvement or maintenance of distance could be conceptualized as the effective component of psychotherapy. However, since simple relationships are rarely the case in the complex field of psychology, we would probably have to hypothesize some interaction of lack of involvement with some other element, such as hope, intrinsic motivation to get well, or the imparting of information. This would account for the effectiveness of some minimal involvement types of treatments, such as placebo therapies in which neutral topics are discussed, inclusion on a waiting list, and, more popularly, the numerous telephone/tape counseling services and self-help books and programs.

Implications

What implications does all of this have for the practice of psychotherapy? If we take Sechrest and associates' (1979) advice and implement the treatment in its strongest form, the logical extreme of lack of involvement would be no involvement with a therapist whatsoever. Those who improved under this method would not be referred to as improving from what is commonly termed "spontaneous remission" but would instead be classified as therapy successes, given that the most effective ingredient in psychotherapy, lack of therapist involvement, has been applied in these cases.

Taking a more moderate view and acknowledging the previously mentioned interactional effects, there remain some means for implementing the element of distance in psychotherapy in a more effective manner than is presently being done. For example, psychologists in small towns could commute from other cities in order not to be involved with their patients in everyday life. The number and frequency of sessions could be decreased. Perhaps screens could even be erected in psychologists' offices to make their lack of involvement a still more potent factor.

In the seemingly endless search for the effective element in psychotherapy, perhaps at last we have found the answer in the lack of involvement between therapist and patient. Future work will be required to operationalize lack of therapist involvement and clarify the components of this critical dimension of the psychotherapy process.

References

Cummings, N.A. (1977). Prolonged (ideal) versus short-term (realistic) psychotherapy. *Professional Psychology, 8,* 419–501.

Cummings, N.A., & Follette, W.T. (1976). Brief psychotherapy and medical utilization. In H. Dörken & Associates (Eds.), *The professional psychologist today.* San Francisco: Jossey-Bass Publishers, 165–174.

Eysenck, H.J. (1952). The effects of psychotherapy: An evaluation. *Journal of Consulting Psychology, 16,* 317–324.

Follette, W.T., & Cummings, N.A. (1967). Psychiatric services and medical utilization in a prepaid health plan setting: Part I. *Medical Care, 5,* 25–35.

Garfield, S.L. (1978). Research on client variables in psychotherapy. In S.L. Garfield & A.E. Bergin (Eds.), *Handbook of psychotherapy and behavior change.* New York: Wiley, 191–232.

Lambert, M.J., Bergin, A.E., & Collins, J.L. (1977). Therapist-induced deterioration in psychotherapy. In A.S. Gurman & A.M. Razin (Eds.), *Effective psychotherapy: A handbook of research.* Elmsford, New York: Pergamon Press, 452–481.

Rachman, S. (1971). Spontaneous remissions in neurotic disorders. In S. Rachman (Ed.), *The effects of psychotherapy.* Oxford, England: Pergamon Press, 18–41.

Sechrest, L., West, S., Phillips, M.A., Redner, R., & Yeaton, W. (1979). Introduction: Some neglected problems in evaluation research: Strength and integrity of treatments. In L. Sechrest, S. West, M.A. Phillips, R. Redner, & W. Yeaton (Eds.), *Evaluation studies review annual, volume 4.* Beverly Hills: Sage, 15–38.

A Proposal for Eliminating the Chronic Shortage of Mental Health Service Providers: Hounds as Humanists

Wayne R. Bartz, Ph.D.
American River College

Roger E. Volger, Ph.D.
Pomona College

The most recent development at the Institute of Exotica-Erotica-Bullotica is the use of hounds as humanistic psychotherapists. They are ideal because of their natural attributes of unconditional positive regard, warmth, compassion, and the ability to openly express emotion. The eventual widespread acceptance of hounds as humanists will help end an era of chronic shortage of therapists within the mental health profession.

We, at the Institute of Exotica-Erotica-Bullotica, are not the first psychotherapists to note the disparity between idealistic humanistic goals for society and the realistic shortage of therapists needed to help achieve those goals. Since the announcement of our first institute program (Bartz, 1970), there has been continued interest in Bullotica-Therapy (often called "Bull-Therapy," for short). Over the years, we have trained hundreds of Bull-Therapists, but have remained acutely aware of the need for many more. We have come to believe that it is the long and arduous psychotherapy training program, itself, which may be in some way responsible for the shortage of mental health service providers. For instance, the minimum work for a neophyte Bull-Therapist involves *weeks* of study, observation, supervision, and $$$$$$$. Moreover, we understand that some therapeutic approaches take *months* to learn *and* require a college degree besides! Clearly, simply expanding the enrollment size of existing training programs is not the answer to the chronic therapist shortage problem. Fortunately, we have stumbled (literally) upon an innovative and effective solution, a discovery that means the *immediate* availability of a new cadre of helping professionals, therapists who not only serve as ideal examples of the self-actualized individual, but who also have many practical advantages over the conventional humanistic therapist. We propose the use of *hounds as humanists.*

A total break with tradition, our discovery may initially sound alarming, but we are confident that an unbiased examination of the pros and cons will convince the most doubting skeptic. For example, the importance of openly expressing feelings is well known, yet years of negative socialization puts many of us right out of touch with our true feelings. In stark contrast, hounds universally express their feelings quite naturally. They do not repress, suppress, or deny, but give clear outward expression to all emotion via tail-wagging, licking, howling, and whining. Most important, this new group of therapists is characterized by an innate ability to consistently express unconditional positive regard, an attribute widely recognized in the popular label, "Man's best friend." In short, hounds naturally and without need of training or personal therapy possess the essential trait of a true humanistic therapist: loving, accepting openness.

Nuts and bolts training problems and expenses are minimal. Unlike traditional psychology graduate students, who tend to bog down in intellectualization and scientism, our new therapists intuitively are able to break free of the confining limits imposed by the tired scientific method. They rarely ask embarrassing questions, such as "What is your operational definition?" They never waste time designing experiments, nor do they petulantly pester supervisors with demands for "data" (whatever that means). Few even own a statistics book and we have yet to see one programming a computer. In short, they have the basic open intellectual and philosophical outlook so essential to the good humanist. The actual cost of training is markedly reduced compared to traditional university programs, since grants and assistantships are unnecessary—just a few weeks of cheap dogfood and they are ready to begin work. (In contrast, graduate students have been known to require years of cheap dogfood.)

An additional plus is that our new therapists are the only candidates we have ever encountered (excuse the pun) who are instantly comfortable in nude therapy. Their totally uninhibited approach is often just the catalyst needed to relax the neophytes entering a nude group (we have noted that a hound licking its genitals is a real icebreaker).

Scheduling therapy hours for hounds is remarkably easy. They rarely demand prime time vacations and are available on call, without reluctance, 24 hours a day, making them great for emergency crisis intervention. (However, they are not recommended for telephone hot-lines). An added bonus beyond scheduling ease is that hounds work even cheaper than marriage-family therapists (most of whom demand more than an occasional doggy-bone).

Innovation often breeds further innovation. One of the noteworthy offshoots of our hound discovery is the "humanist in your home" program. Our clients take their therapist home during difficult periods for a modest rental fee ($5.00 per day—a marked savings over sending out a social worker). When the client returns home after a hard day's work, our therapist waits with open paws at the door. Love, under-standing, compassion, unconditional positive regard—all the essentials for a meaningful relationship are instantly available. Crass as it may sound, a further advantage is that clients can purchase these remarkable therapists. For example, particularly unactualized clients can take a wholesome hound home permanently for an intense, long-term, live-in experience (we call it "life-therapy").

As with any innovative therapeutic method, there are some disad-vantages to hounds as humanists, but the list is pleasantly short. First, institutional budget directors have sometimes expressed reluctance to purchase essential work materials, such as Milkbones, dog chow, flea powder, and worm pills. However, we have discovered that, if it is made very clear in purchase orders that these supplies are required for humanistic therapists, they are rarely questioned.

Because of their open expression of emotion, particularly joy, hu-manist-hounds sometimes, unfortunately, manifest the intensity of feel-ings by peeing on the floor. This occurs about twice as often with hounds as it does with our regular therapists. We handle both situations in the same way: push their noses in it. Another practical concern is that hounds are, by nature, quite hairy, and a failure to bathe regularly can lead to atmospheric problems in small therapy rooms. However, the fact is that hounds, today, are generally less hairy than most of our regular humanistic therapists, and many clients have actually ex-pressed a clear preference for the hounds in tight quarters.

A minor disadvantage with hounds is the occasional use of ques-tionable judgment in responding to important therapeutic material. They may interrupt a client in mid-sentence with a sloppy lick across the mouth and have been observed to curl up and fall asleep in the midst of gut-spilling revelations. Even more disconcerting, at certain periods in their lives, hounds have an upsetting tendency to impulsively hump the legs of clients during or after therapy sessions. Most regular humanistic therapists are much more accurate and rarely hit just legs.

A word of caution concerning particular hounds. We have found that the almost total lack of responsiveness and minimal signs of life in Bassett Hounds limits their suitability for working with all but the most animated clients, who thrive with little therapist feedback. For this reason, we are exploring the Bassett Hound's effectiveness in psychoanalytic therapy and the use of other breeds where they might be naturally well-suited. For example, we are finding Dobermans to be excellent as behavior therapists (for obvious reasons) and Chihuahuas seem to work well as Rational-Emotive therapists. The possibilities boggle the mind.

The Institute staff believe that the unique problems of our new approach will, in time, be fully overcome. We are confident that most open-minded therapists will agree that these compassionate and feeling therapists are indeed ideal models of perfect personhood. This untapped resource of canine therapists could eventually help us attain the ultimate humanistic goals of universal self-actualization, love, riches, harmony, health, world peace, and a good 25 cent beer.

References

Bartz, W.R. (1970). Summer program: Institute of Exotica-Erotica-Bullotica. *Worm Runner's Digest, 12,* 66–67.

A Unifying Theory of the Psychotherapies: Advice Therapy

John W. Zuboy, Ed.D.
Davis & Elkins College

The medium and long-term outcome for those patients who received treatment was no different for those who were provided simply with advice.
—Rachman and Wilson (1980)

Taking a cue from Rachman and Wilson's (1980) work, the author reports in this paper a radically new approach to psychotherapeutic intervention—Advice Therapy (AT). Advice Therapy is based on the simple proposition that our population is becoming increasingly incapable of independent thought and action in every arena of life. There is abundant anecdotal evidence supporting this contention, viz., Ann Landers, college students, Yuppies, Jerry Falwell, test scores, public schools, Congress, the Sun Belt, etc. Clearly, PEOPLE NEED TO BE TOLD THE WHO, WHAT, WHEN, WHERE, AND WHY of their lives.

The author is aware that, at first glance, this position may seem incompatible with many of the major psychotherapeutic approaches to helping people. However, the author feels that this is primarily a problem in semantics and hopes to illustrate, below, how these approaches can be subsumed by the over-riding principle of AT.

Rogerian Advice Therapy (RAT)

This is, perhaps, the most difficult theory of all to integrate with the principles of AT. The trick, here, is to have a profound empathic understanding of just how the client is screwed up. From such an understanding, it follows that you will know what is best for the person, but you must loudly and frequently deny that you do. Finally, the most important rule that must remain inviolate is that the advice must always be preceded with *reflective camouflage statements (RCS)*. For example, if you believe the client is not firm enough in disciplining his children, at the first opportunity you might try the following RCS: "*You* seem to feel that your kids are ungrateful brats and would like to take a parenting course to learn to discipline them."

Humanistic-Existential Advice Therapy (HEAT)

This approach is a cousin to RAT, but much more direct (no need for camouflage here). In fact, the therapist must be fully and genuinely present for the client and willing to use his "self as an instrument" to repair the person. Practitioners of this persuasion will use the "I (know what is best for) Thou" approach. The "tough/tender" principle is fundamental to HEAT treatment. The therapist must model authentic, spontaneous behavior in reaction to the client. It is generally best to demonstrate the "tender" (approving, accepting, celebrating, applauding, etc.) behaviors first. This should be overdone with great zeal and abandon, bordering on poor impulse control. The implied message should be "I am also willing to disclose my tough emotions with you," including rage, disgust, contempt, pity, indifference, loathing, disappointment, etc. When done properly, this tacit threat is usually effective in inducing the client to genuinely embrace the necessary advice.

Music Art Dance Advice Therapy (MAD AT)

In MAD AT, the therapist encourages the appropriate creative expression. This generally makes the client feel good but, of course, has little to do with the advice to be dispensed. The clever MAD AT clinician simply assigns an arbitrary, but plausible, interpretation to the expressive product, in the service of the preordained advice. This modality is really catching on at state hospitals and on college campuses.

Primal Advice Therapy (PAT)

Primal Advice Therapy works on a variation of the "soft cop/hard cop" principle. At the initiation of therapy, the therapist assumes a kindly, gentle manner. He advises the client to abstain from the practices that serve defensive ends, such as drinking, smoking, eating, television, sex, reading, human contact, etc. Ordinarily, clients comply to some degree in order to please the therapist. Of course, to the degree that they comply, the clients are raw and wired out. This is the time for the "tough cop" to make his appearance. The therapist now abruptly switches to a Synanon style of encounter. The dissonance this produces, coupled with the already vulnerable state of the client, sets the scene for the therapeutic moment—the therapist *SCREAMS* advice, succinctly and repetitiously, until the client spontaneously begins to scream the advice at himself. This should proceed until exhaustion sets in. At this point, RAT reflective camouflage statements are useful to help the client internalize and consolidate the advice.

Erhard Advice Therapy: Intensive Training (EAT IT)

The EAT IT gambit is to make the clients guess the advice. This leads to so much frustration that they accelerate their exploratory behavior in an attempt to "get it." Never acknowledge their efforts, simply tell them that they will know AT when they get AT. Naturally, at the same time you are covertly reinforcing those behaviors that approximate your advice agenda. Practitioners of this approach receive a 25% discount in their malpractice insurance because of the strong "deniability" position inherent in it.

Bioenergetics Advice Therapy: Intra Tuning (BEAT IT)

BEAT IT employs a variation of the old "foot in the door" strategem. The therapist subjects the client to the most painful and humiliating of the Bioenergetic exercises. He literally requires the client to prostrate himself on the altar of therapy, lays on hands in a dominant manner, and suggests there are multitudinous, somewhat sinister/sexually repressed experiences that the patient knows nothing about. Having gone that far, it is easy, in fact a relief, for the client to comply with mere verbal advice.

Gestalt Advice Therapy (GAT)

GAT works on a triple twist. The therapist must strongly convey the message that (1) advice is never given, (2) if it were given, the therapist (in the words of a true Gestaltist) wouldn't "give a shit" if it were taken, and (3) if it were taken, the therapist would be in no way responsible for the outcome. The primary function of the therapist is to direct the attention of the client to the obvious, in the here and now, to produce awareness. The direction, of course, implies advice. As in EAT IT, the client gropes desperately for confirmation of his insight. If he is off the mark, the therapist gives some nonverbal clue, such as opening a book and beginning to read, or lighting a cigarette and blowing smoke disdainfully into the face of the client. If the client is on the mark, the therapist simply says, "ya."

Conclusion

These are a few examples of the way the author envisions Advice Therapy accomplishing the unifying task. Of course, there is no end to it. Who will be the next theorist to develop Transactional Advice Therapy (TAT), or even Drug Advice Therapy (DAT)? There is much work to be done to explicate these and other approaches further.

References

Rachman, S.J., & Wilson, G.T. (1980). *The effects of psychological therapy.* Oxford: Pergamon Press, 4.

Cognitive-Behavioral Treatment of Chronic Flatulence

Perry Stalsis, Ph.D.

Flatulence is a complex socio-psycho-biological phenomenon which may be viewed as a form of interpersonal communication or meta-communication (Cheese & Cutter, 1977). Many individuals wish to enhance their ability to predict and control this phenomenon. Some individuals wish to reduce the frequency of their flatulence episodes, particularly their unpredictable flatulence episodes.

However, the Flatulence Aptitude Repertoire Test reveals that 53% of all Introductory Psychology students have flatulence skill deficits and most of these students have requested training in assertive flatulence (P.U. Plenty, 1983).

The Training

The 10-session training program was administered by an experienced flatulence therapist, whom the subjects nicknamed "Windbreaker." Training consisted of modeling, aromatic restructuring, and olfactory feedback.

For homework assignments, each student kept a "Flatulence Diary," recording all flatulence episodes: eliciting stimuli, response characteristics, and environmental consequences.

Subjects

Subjects were limited to primary, chronic flatulence, excluding all cases of acute flatulence and flatulence secondary to another syndrome, such as Vegetarian Personality Disorder.

In addition, subjects were put on a vegetable-free diet for seven days prior to the beginning of training. As Albert Bandura has pointed out in *Principles of Behavior Modification* (1969, p. 296): "Beans, beans, the musical fruit; the more you eat the more you toot!"

Outcome Measures

Behavioral ratings were made by three judges who were trained to evaluate each flatulence episode on the following dimensions: 1) Duration; 2) Loudness; 3) Pitch; 4) Tonal Quality; and 5) Fragrance. The judges indicated their evaluations by holding up a placard displaying a numeral ranging from "1" (lowest rating) to "10" (highest rating).

Subjects were also informally interviewed on their reactions to the research. The reaction of a subject known as "Boomer" was typical: "I believe that this is a very important and long neglected area of research," he said. "I was really blown away by it."

Results

Unfortunately, three of the 20 subjects left without explanation in the middle of the first session. Ten more subjects and two judges left rather abruptly during the second session. No one (not even the trainer) showed up for the third session.

Discussion

It is clear that more rigorously designed research is required, since the present study yielded no results at all. It is suggested that the lack of any outcome data in the present study may be partially due to the fact that the research was conducted indoors and in a rather small room with little ventilation. Future research should probably be conducted out-of-doors and subjects, judges, and trainers might be provided with anesthetizing nasal spray.

A Great Moment in Gestalt Psychotherapy

Kirk E. Farnsworth, Ph.D.
Trinity College

Client: Do you think I'm crazy?

Therapist: Change that question into a statement.

Client: I think I'm going nuts. I must learn to control myself.

Therapist: Control yourself? What are you, two different people?

Client: Change that question into a statement.

Therapist: Shut up! When I want you to play the therapist, I'll let you know.

Client: I give up. I've got a headache and my mind is blank, so I can't talk anymore.

Therapist: That's no good. Say, "I am choosing to have a headache rather than talk to you," "I'm blocking and I take responsibility for that," and "I don't want to"—not "I can't."

Client: Geez—what are you trying to do to me? I've never met anyone like you before! (pounds fist on chair)

Therapist: There is some expression going on there; don't interrupt it.

Client: (continues to pound fist)

Therapist: Who is it you want to hit?

Client: You!

Therapist: Okay. Now put me in this empty chair and hit me . . . no, stupid, the *empty* chair . . . no, stop . . .

Behavioral Strategies for Coping with Urban Crime: Vigilante Effectiveness Training (V.E.T.)

Michael F. Shaughnessy, Ph.D.
Eastern New Mexico University

Effectiveness training has become an integral part of contemporary psychology, with workshops being offered in parent, teacher, leader, and communication training. As the incidence of violent, aggressive, and assaultive crimes increases, particularly in urban settings, still another area of effectiveness training appears to be urgently needed, namely, Vigilante Effectiveness Training (V.E.T.). The present paper presents a model for Vigilante Effectiveness Training and proposes areas for further research and exploration in this new and developing area of psychology.

Violent, not to mention serious, crime in urban America has reached epidemic proportions, according to the most recent study of Data (1985) available. As more and more people have a bad personal experience with being raped, robbed, and/or murdered, they have looked to the overworked police departments of America for protection, only to find the police seemingly ineffectual in stemming the tides of crime. Citizens, subjected to the ever present threats of crime, find themselves living in a constant state of fear, anxiety, stress, tension, dread, helplessness, hopelessness, despair, and, to some extent, unhappiness, as well. What seems clearly called for, then, is some form of intervention strategy to restore to America's citizenry a feeling of being an active agent in protecting themselves from senseless crimes and uncalled for bodily harm. Based on the latest work of Goetz (1985), and extrapolating from the previous pioneering work of Gordon (1970, 1974, 1977), the author presents, here, a proposal for Vigilante Effectiveness Training

(V.E.T.), outlining the beauty of its parsimonious approach to crime prevention, and highlighting research areas ripe for further investigation.

Basic Components of V.E.T.

Personality Characteristics

The successful vigilante must come to training possessing certain personality traits. While a vindictive nature can be developed during training, a sense of injustice and lack of faith in the judicial system is imperative right from the start. Cynicism for attorneys and a negativistic attitude toward bleeding heart liberal judges is basic to the vigilante position. A natural propensity toward preparedness is a good predictor of successful V.E.T. outcome, thus the resourceful vigilante-to-be comes to his first V.E.T. session armed with a gun, knife, tear gas canisters, and hand grenades.

Standard Issue Weaponry

Weaponry is another component of V.E.T. The purchase of unmarked guns, and the loading and aiming of a Smith and Wesson or .357 Magnum are a major part of V.E.T. Just as rapists are concerned about "penetration," so too is the effective vigilante. Citizen band radios, too, are of standard issue, allowing the vigilante to monitor police channels in order to facilitate contacts and interventions with criminals.

Battle Uniform

The wardrobe of the vigilante must be considered. As Molloy (1975) has indicated, one must "dress for success," i.e., one should wear a bullet proof vest for protection. Sunglasses, exemplified by Clint Eastwood and Charles Bronson, may also be worn. Steel tipped shoes can be worn for kicking muggers, punks, perverts, and rapists when they are down.

Basic Training and Field Exercises

The streets of large cities make a great natural training field for practicing Vigilante Effectiveness Training. The vigilante-in-training is sent off into traffic in a car to await being cut off by a car whose driver does not use turn signals. Bullets can be fired into the offending auto's gas tank and one's horn can be leaned on extensively, providing negative reinforcement so that proper behaviors can be taught, and hopefully learned.

Physical training is, of course, rigorous and grueling. Biofeedback is utilized to reduce high blood pressure, anxiety, and tension, all of which, if gone unchecked, can lead to an unsteady trigger finger. Desensitization is used to diminish any superego conflict in novice vigilantes. Cognitive training is employed so that vigilantes can tell what their apprehended muggers are cognating. Thus, insight into "flight or fight" phenomenon is taught. In addition, communication skills are taught so that the vigilante can speak with "innocent until proven guilty" souls possessing bloody knives and smoking guns in their hands.

Typical beginning verbal intervention strategies for the vigilante include, "I know what you're thinking, punk," "Go ahead—MAKE MY DAY," and (for off-duty policemen), "no trial—no reports to file" and "a man's got to know his limitations." The above comments, of course, can also serve as secret passwords to enter vigilante group therapy meetings (if any are needed to discuss common concerns about mass criminal conspiracies).

The vigilante should have a supply of illicit drugs, to be placed or planted on their victims. Heroin, cocaine, "Angel Dust," marijuana, and L.S.D., alone or in combination, are excellent drugs for planting on victims.

As the police typically try to construct a psychological profile of killers, the vigilante must take care to leave misleading clues when engaging in "surgical removal" of undesirables so as to provide for a false profile. Texts such as Janov's (1970) *The Primal Scream* and any issue of the *Journal of Polymorphous Perversity* can be left at the scene of judicial intervention to confuse authorities.

Visual pattern recognition is an important part of V.E.T., as the vigilante-in-training is taught to become adept in spotting muggers on the street and identifying hoods and punks in slimy sections of the city. Black leather jackets, switchblades, and black turtle neck sweaters are "dead" give-aways. In advanced V.E.T., the vigilante-to-be is able to spot law breakers by simple eye contact.

Park walking at night not only provides fresh air, but allows vigilantes to form new friendships with recently released murderers out "on-bond" or those killers recently freed due to "minor legal technicalities." V.E.T. provides information on finding parks and determining which parks to frequent. Behavioral charting is taught with baseline and various treatment procedures. Treatment "A" includes being dressed as a member of the opposite sex, and Treatment "B" includes dressing in a three piece suit so as to lure robbers into confrontation of "your money or your life." Of course, intervention during the baseline period is an acceptable component of V.E.T.

At V.E.T. meetings, the rights of all vigilantes are scrupulously reviewed. These include the right to make a citizen's arrest, and the right to go to a baseball or softball game with a baseball bat in hand. Also taught are travel skills necessary for survival. Our crusaders of justice learn subway riding at night, surviving on a Greyhound or Trailways bus, and traversing large cities such as Chicago and Detroit. Coping with bus terminals and bathrooms in bus terminals is a separate training component of V.E.T. and much too extensive to be examined in an introductory article. In addition, travel to local American Civil Liberties Union conventions is a high point of the V.E.T. training.

Identification of possible sites for vigilante action is another integral part of training. Local Seven-Eleven stores, 24-hour Stop N' Shops, and all night gas stations are all examined and sites for intervention are specified.

In case of apprehension by law enforcement officers, stress inoculation training is also offered in V.E.T. The stress inoculation program prepares vigilantes for grueling police interrogations, for coping with possible perverted cell mates and unhygienic conditions (e.g., rats, vermin, mice) during incarceration, and for further pre-trial "plea bargaining" so as to obtain probation. Training in negotiating with lawyers for movie rights, book rights, t.v. rights, and serial rights is also offered.

In order to procure an "innocent by reason of insanity" verdict, training is offered in the new *Diagnostic and Statistical Manual of Mental Disorders* (American Psychiatric Association, 1980), so that one may feign mental disturbance and appear disoriented in all three spheres, manifest flat blunted affect, and imitate symptoms of organicity.

A final minor training module is offered in proselytizing others to vigilanteism. Any V.E.T. graduate can solicit others to the new skill and "joy of vigilanteism." Special guidelines are offered for liberal democrats and Yuppies.

Future Training

In the future, V.E.T. will offer more specialized training to help vigilantes cope with specific problem groups, e.g., Hare Krishna singers, street peddlers, street clowns and mimes, and other unsavory elements in our society. Coping tactics for liberal judges will also be offered. Training in karate, judo, and other martial arts will enable the vigilante to quickly, cleanly, and effectively perform his work without having to resort to handguns, the bane of our society.

Finally, it is anticipated that V.E.T. training centers will spring up in major cities across the United States and become as American as Howard Johnson's and the Golden Arches. It is predicted that V.E.T. will take its place in the annals of American history, right along side of I.B.M., the C.I.A., and the F.B.I. Tapes and workshops on vigilante tactics and techniques will appear across our nation and, in all probability, a "Journal of Vigilanteism" will soon be published.

Implications for Future Research

The empirical research into the effectiveness of V.E.T. has not, as yet, been documented. The personality of the effective vigilante needs examination and the various methodologies utilized in training must be systematically explored. Meta-analysis and multivariate procedures must be employed in order to concisely specify intervening variables which may interfere with effective training. In summary, just as Parent Effectiveness Training (P.E.T.), Teacher Effectiveness Training (T.E.T.), and Leader Effectiveness Training (L.E.T.) have been subjected to rigorous methodological examination and study, so too must Vigilante Effectiveness Training (V.E.T.) be statistically and experimentally examined. It is hoped that this research will be conducted in the near future and that professional ethics committees will be dealt with in a manner consistent with vigilanteism.

References

American Psychiatric Association (1980). *Diagnostic and statistical manual of mental disorders, 3rd edition.* Washington, D.C.: American Psychiatric Association.

Data, W. (1985). *An empirical assessment of crime in America: I wouldn't go outside, if I were you.* New York: The Bernhard Goetz Foundation.

Goetz, B.H. (1985). *An experimental study (with three replications) of crime reduction on an urban transportation system.* New York: in press.

Gordon, T. (1970). *Parent effectiveness training.* New York: Plume.

Gordon, T. (1974). *Teacher effectiveness training.* New York: Wyden.
Gordon, T. (1977). *Leader effectiveness training.* New York: Wyden.
Janov, A. (1970). *The primal scream.* New York: Dell.
Molloy, J.T. (1975). *Dress for success.* New York: Wyden.

Thanatotherapy: A One-Session Approach to Brief Psychotherapy

Kathleen M. Donald, Ph.D.
University of North Carolina

Bruce E. Wampold, Ph.D.
University of Oregon

Given that most psychotherapies acknowledge the grave responsibility for curing the patient as efficiently as possible, the current trend toward brief psychotherapy clearly indicates the profession's commitment to limiting the length and curtailing the cost of therapy. Although many therapists are dead-set against abbreviating the therapy process (not to mention the profits), even those private practitioners who charge exorbitant hourly fees will admit there are certain patients whom they wish would not return after the initial session, despite the loss of revenue. Typically diagnosed as borderline personalities, these patients are notorious for late-night irrelevant "emergency" phone calls, no common sense, no redeeming qualities, no income, and no health insurance. The therapist who undertakes to treat these patients must be prepared to deal with suicidal tendencies, both the patient's and his/her own. Although Thanatotherapy was originally designed with these particular patients in mind, it is applicable to a wide range of psychological disorders.

Historical Precedents

Although prehistoric evidence of suicide as treatment is sketchy (Sketchy, 1980), the first written record of this approach in the alleviation of problem behavior occurred during the Classical period in Greece. So familiar is the story of Socrates' self-administration of poison that the term Socratic Method (sometimes referred to as the Hemlock Maneuver) is commonly used to indicate behavioral self-control via suicide (Zorba, 1966).

In general, Eastern cultures, with their age-old traditional acceptance of this mode of treatment, have made more technical advances than their Western counterparts (Seppuku & Harakiri, 1979). However, it must be mentioned that certain eras of Western civilization provided a fertile climate for the cultivation of treatment by suicide, most probably because it was preferred to the alternatives of that particular period. For instance, when compared to being devoured by a hungry lion in the arena, burned at the stake, stoned to death, or crucified, it is obvious why hordes of would-be early Christian martyrs chose suicide. Likewise, during the Middle Ages, many a peasant selected suicide in lieu of bubonic plague, serfdom, thumb screws, witch trials, the rack, the Iron Maiden, or the Inquisition (Cafflick, 1985).

Current Developments

In the 20th century, Kamikaze (1941) jumped the gun on his contemporaries in military experimentation with brief treatment and brought back to life what had been a dead issue in psychology for years. The most recent development along this line is the approach called Thanatotherapy. This radical new treatment brings to full flower Freud's much-maligned and little-understood concept of the death wish. Although Freud was on the right track, he became obsessed with Eros and failed to devote sufficient attention to Thanatos. With Thanatotherapy, the "sine qua non" of treatment becomes the death wish, the elicitation of which leads to self-actualization "in extremis."

The key to successful application of Thanatotherapy techniques depends, as with all treatment modalities, on the skill of the therapist. Not only must the Thanatotherapist facilitate the execution of the death wish, he/she must also cultivate an attitude of unconditional negative regard (de Sade, 1780) to create the optimal therapeutic ambiance. Usually, the assumption of a deadpan expression on the therapist's face will create an adequately aversive atmosphere for a favorable Thanatotherapeutic encounter (Sourpuss, 1983).

The Thanatotherapist must be prepared to personalize the treatment to fit the patient's diagnosis. For instance, with compulsive personalities, it is important to allow time for excessive list making and to rehearse with the client every detail of the plan. With hysterics, details are less important so long as a dramatic, attention-getting method is selected. The schizophrenic is more likely to respond to bizarre methodologies, such as overdosing on Mrs. Paul's Fish Sticks or reruns of "Love Boat." The most successful tack to take with paranoids is to utilize a variant of traditional Voodoo, instilling in the patient's mind the unerring belief that, by means of a vicious Communist plot, his or her life is doomed unless 200,000 MX missiles are installed (Whinebugger,

1985). Phobics are taught behaviors that will scare them to death, although many are gun-shy of treatment. Those with anxiety disorders are instructed how to alter their thinking so they can worry to death. The most efficient treatment of psychopaths, particularly antisocial personalities, is Thanato-Group (T-Group) Therapy.[1] Occasionally, T-Group Therapy is also effective with multiple personalities. Dependent personalities often require assistance in the execution of their treatment plans; however, the Thanatotherapist must be careful not to get roped in. With bulimics and alcoholics, compliance is usually enhanced by inviting them to an all-you-can-eat-or-drink "Whine and Jeez" party, in order to inspire the correct negative mind set. As might be expected, malingerers pose special problems and have to be forced to complete treatment. For obvious reasons, the individual with a martyr complex responds most readily to this mode of therapy and rarely needs coaching or encouragement.

When treating recalcitrant patients who resist a straightforward, skill-building approach, the Thanatotherapist may have more success with indirect, Ericksonian-type metaphors, such as, "Why not give it a shot?" or "Jump at the chance" or "Bite the bullet." If all else fails, the use of a Thanatotherapeutic Double Bind is indicated, such as: "The choice is yours; life can be a bitter pill to swallow or it can be a blast."

Advantages of Thanatotherapy

There are many important advantages of Thanatotherapy. First, the Thanatotherapist can handle a larger caseload because of the quick turnover of clientele. As a result, therapy is made more stimulating, although not more lively, as the therapist greets and treats a greater number of interesting individuals. Second, Thanatotherapy encourages the active participation of the patient in his/her own treatment (Colt, 1945), thereby minimizing the development of an overly dependent transference relationship. Third, termination issues are simplified and dealt with early on in treatment, typically in the intake session. Premature termination is a virtual impossibility. Fourth, Thanatotherapy, as opposed to most brief therapies, is a permanent solution. Our research

---

[1] Thanato-Group (T-Group) Therapy with antisocial personalities most typically begins with Group Homicide Therapy; however, Individual Thanatotherapy is recommended for the remaining group member. For the life of us, we cannot understand why some lay individuals (usually the warden) oppose Thanatotherapy while at the same time advocating capital punishment (Mouse, 1985).

has shown that, when executed correctly, there is a negligible recidivism rate. Thanatotherapy essentially eliminates the revolving-door syndrome notorious in mental health circles (Noose & Pilz, 1983). Fifth, patients are immensely satisfied with Thanatotherapy. Using a methodology adapted from that used by the American Tobacco Institute, in a survey of over 2,000 patients treated with Thanatotherapy, few patients complained, although it must be noted that the return rate was low. Sixth, Thanatotherapy is a culturally unbiased approach, a one-shot treatment that is effective with all diagnoses. Seventh, Thanatotherapy reduces the possibility of unethical behavior on the part of the therapist, although necrophiliac therapists are ill-advised to adopt this modality. Finally, third-party payments that limit coverage for psychotherapy are not problematic (remember that patients should sign the insurance form before the session begins).

Disadvantages of Thanatotherapy

Before undertaking this new approach, there are some caveats for the practitioner to consider. First, it is important for the therapist, especially those in private practice, to make arrangements for payment in advance. Second, the clinician cannot count on word-of-mouth referrals as is possible with less radical treatments. Unless patients leave behind a note, referrals from past patients usually will be infrequent. Third, research with this population is difficult due to major threats to internal validity (viz., mortality) and to poor response rates to follow-up studies, although the empty chair technique can be useful here. Finally, the therapist should be aware of countertransference, lest he or she overdose on the treatment.

Case Study

Dr. X has been in private practice for four years and shares office space with three other psychologists. On a Thursday the receptionist received a call from Ms. Fit, requesting an appointment with Dr. X. The receptionist explained that Dr. X was leaving for vacation on the following Saturday morning for five weeks and would not be able to see any additional patients until his return. When Ms. Fit explained that it was an emergency, the receptionist suggested that she make an appointment with one of the other psychologists. This was not satisfactory to Ms. Fit because Dr. X had been recommended by her present therapist, Dr. X's ex-wife; ironically, Ms. Fit explained that "Dr. X is the only one who can save my life." Dr. X declined to speak with her.

Thursday evening, Ms. Fit called Dr. X at home; apparently she had obtained his unlisted number from his stockbroker. Although Dr. X initially refused to speak with her, on the fourth call, around 2:00 a.m., he agreed to talk to her and obtained the following information. Ms. Fit had previously seen six therapists, two of whom subsequently benefited immensely from Thanatotherapy themselves. Although married three times, Ms. Fit currently was without partner, friends, or family. All 12 of her children had run away from home before age six. She had been hospitalized 42 times in the past year and had had 13 surgeries, although she reported that none had helped her. She supported herself on welfare, living on the street and spending most of her income on alcohol. She had "successfully" completed nine alcohol rehabilitation programs. Ms. Fit informed Dr. X that she really didn't need therapy but just wanted a friend she could talk to, day or night. Dr. X agreed to see her at eight o'clock Friday morning. Ms. Fit called Dr. X three more times during the night, alternating between hysteria, depression, and aggression (claiming she would kill him, if he terminated the conversation).

Recognizing the clear indications that Thanatotherapy was the treatment of choice for Ms. Fit, Dr. X skillfully intervened during the 8:00 a.m. appointment, which took place at 10:00 a.m. because Ms. Fit overslept (and which, incidentally, dictated that a paying patient be rescheduled). Dr. X was able to respond with antipathy to each of Ms. Fit's statements. She grew more and more angry and threatened to kill both of them. Dr. X suggested that she begin with herself, a suggestion that resulted in the successful implementation of Thanatotherapy. Dr. X was able to have his vacation without incident. He had no additional contacts with Ms. Fit, although he did receive a thank-you note from his ex-wife.

Conclusion

Psychology has seen a plethora of approaches to treating dysfunctional populations. Thanatotherapy is meant to be the final word on this subject. Anyone who doubts the effectiveness of this treatment is welcome to visit our laboratory to receive an introductory session. Demonstrations with confederate clients generally are not advisable.

References

Cafflick, H.R. (1985). Is the vocation of martyrdom still a viable career option in the "Me Generation"? *The Annals of Papal Bull, 193,* 1733–1749.

Colt, B.B. (1945). How to safely kill intruders, one's children, or oneself with handguns. *Journal of the National Rifle Association, 12,* 1–10.

de Sade, M. (1780). If looks could kill. *Journal of Client-Centered Sadism, 5,* 173–175.

Kamikaze, D.B. (1941). *Modern approaches to self-actualization.* Tokyo: Bonzai Press.

Mouse, E., III (1985). *How to prevent suicide on death row.* Paper presented at the meeting of the Wardens Association, Washington, D.C.

Noose, H.M., & Pilz, O.D. (1983). *Is the mental health center a dead end?* Oslo, Norway: Lemming Press.

Seppuku, J.C., & Harakiri, E.E. (1979). *The way out is the way out.* Osaka: Osaka Tumi Press.

Sketchy, H.W. (1980). The bison as symbol of suicide: A reinterpretation of paleolithic animal imagery in the caves of Lascaux and Altamira. *Acta Anthropologica Absurda, 103,* 1–633.

Sourpuss, U.R. (1983). *Physiognomy and therapy: Face the facts.* Philadelphia: Friendly Press.

Whinebugger, C. (1985). *The collective unconscious is paranoid.* Washington, D.C.: Classified Document (eyes only).

Zorba, G. (1966). The hemlock maneuver: The hug of death. *Journal of Radical, Outrageous Emergency Treatment, 13,* 7–11.

2
Psychoanalysis

The Nasal Complex and Other Recent Advances in Psychoanalytic Theory

Perry Stalsis, Ph.D.

The brilliance of the early psychoanalytic thinkers enabled them to identify the oral, anal, and phallic stages of psychosexual development. It has been left to later workers, however, to note Freud's greatest omission, the nasal stage, which occurs between the anal and phallic stages of development.

Perhaps the most traumatic step in the socialization of the young child, the nasal stage is initiated by the parental demand that the child blow its nose into a handkerchief and "Quit that awful sniffling." A nasal fixation occurs when the child's nasal training is too harsh, too lenient, both, or neither.

Throughout history, myths of every culture have contained many elements which are nothing more than thinly disguised representations of unresolved nasal libido. For example: Pinocchio, Cyrano de Bergerac, and the midget in the nudist colony who kept getting his nose in everyone's business.

Freud (1923d) correctly noted that a request for a cosmetic nose job is a defense against depression, which is a defense against aggression, which is a defense against sexuality. However, Freud made a significant error when he accepted at face value the fact that all little boys have sexual intercourse with their mommies every morning as soon as daddy leaves for the office. He failed to see that this "sexual" ejaculation is nothing but a symbolic derivative of the boy's archetypical longing for his mother to blow his nose.

One of my own patients was an otherwise attractive young woman whose nose seriously interfered with her love life. Suffice it to say that no man would date her because it was physically impossible to kiss her on the mouth. Her nose job led to an active social life, followed by a happy marriage and three children who brought her great joy.

It is obvious that her analysis must be judged a total failure. The surgeon's operating table was nothing but a symbolic substitute for the analytic couch, and the operation was simply another manifestation of her profound resistance to resolving her unconscious nasal complex.

Vagina Envy

It is now definitely known that one of the most powerful masculine instincts is vagina envy. Proof of the biological superiority of women is their vagina, which, during sexual intercourse, surrounds and dominates the pathetic male organ, and frequently causes it permanent injury.

At other times the male penis just hangs there, feeble and vulnerable, while the female vagina is protected and secure within her body.

The ever-more-powerful weapons which men have traditionally carried into battle are clearly a reaction formation against the male's profound feelings of genital inferiority. These feelings are so strong that the male has attempted to overcome his organ inferiority by the foolish and unnecessary defense mechanism of growing several inches taller than the female.

It is true that certain psychologists have presented cultural, or even biological, explanations for masculine aggressiveness. But these theories (unsupported by clinical intuition) are nothing more than a reflection of their resistance against recognizing their own vagina envy and thus support, rather than refute, the discovery of vagina envy.

Are Heterosexuals Sick?

In recent years the analytic literature has carried a lively debate on the nature of heterosexuality: choice or disease?

Those who hold that heterosexuality is a disease point out that heterosexuality produces babies, and only a sick person would want to bring more people into a world that doesn't even have enough psychoanalysts to treat the present population.

On the other side of this issue are an equal number of scholars who hold that heterosexual intercourse is not sick, but merely disgusting. These theorists point out that intercourse is a repetitious, monotonous activity that makes the bed smell like fish and interferes with more civilized pursuits, such as earning money to pay for your analyst's next trip to Europe. But, they argue, people are free to choose heterosexual intercourse, just as they are free to pick their nose (see above) or break wind at the dinner table (Stalsis, in press).

Summary

Clinical experience has shown that people who disagree with these discoveries are homosexuals and their next tax return will be carefully scrutinized by the I.R.S.

A Modern Day Psychoanalytic Fable

Alma H. Bond, Ph.D.

Institute for Psychoanalytic Training and Research

Once upon a time there was a little girl named Cinderella.[1] Now, we all know that Cinderella loved to sit among the ashes and it is hardly necessary in this Freudian Age to trace the source of this behavior in her psychosexual development. What is not well known, however, is that Cinderella had a schizophrenogenic mother and two sisters who were pathologically consumed with jealousy because of unsublimated sibling rivalry.

Cinderella's mother suffered from unresolved symbiotic needs and was very dependent on the good will and affection of her older daughters, so that whenever she felt frustrated by one of them, she drained off her wrath by attacking Cinderella. The sisters cooperated, of course, because they enjoyed getting in their digs at baby sister. This was a very expedient arrangement and made for a smooth running household. It also kept Cindy feeling a bit shaky about herself, so she knocked herself out trying to prove that she was good, unselfish, and worthwhile. This provided free slave labor as well as a scapegoat for Mama and sisters. Of course, it was rather hard on Cinderella, but apparently that did not matter. The whole is more than one of its parts.

Research indicates[2] that the pathologically jealous siblings inflicted on Cinderella "every vexation they could think of, and then made fun of her" for her unhealthy depressive state. But Cindy did not dare to see the truth. Because then they would have accused her of suffering from ideas of reference and delusions of persecution, and suggested that from the clinical point of view, she showed evidence of withdrawal from reality, thought disorder, and bizarre delusions. No girl likes to be reviled, even in the language of psychiatry. So Cindy sat in the ashes and turned her anger against herself. (I think she ground her teeth.)

It must be apparent by now that Cindy's mother was a rather strange lady. The world for her was divided into "her" and "not-her." The "her" portion, at this time comprising herself and two older daughters, was considered inviolate and regal. The "not-her" part (which included Cinderella) was thought toxic and dangerous. This was a neat way of getting rid of all the parts of herself she didn't like. And, of course, no guilt was called for, whatever the action, because Cinderella, *ipso facto,* being part of the "non-her" world, was no good and deserved whatever she got.

Now Cindy couldn't let herself love this schizophrenogenic mother because she had to preserve what ego functions were still intact, such as the ability to wait and tolerate frustration, anticipation of consequence, and fantasy in the place of untimely gratification. And had she let herself care, she would have been too overwhelmed with longing and the constant barrage of assaults to be able to function at all. So, Cindy didn't know that she cared.

Yet somewhere deep inside of her a hazy, fuzzy memory of rich full whiteness was bursting away. Dilemma—what was she to do? She wanted to remember the milk, the rich full warmness of it cosily sloshing inside, but was petrified of further enslavement. So how did she resolve this dilemma? Easy. She split off from consciousness her love for the woman and denied the reality of kinship. (She actually convinced herself that they were stepmother and stepsisters!) Then she used the ego function of denial by fantasy to pull herself up by the bootstraps. But we are running ahead of the plot.

Did you ever notice that Cindy's father is never mentioned in the story? Well, that is because he is a weak, ineffectual man who was castrated (symbolically) by the mother; hence he does not appear in the story. Cinderella (who had latent homosexual tendencies) identified with her father, the only member of the family halfway decent to her, who even tried to rescue her once in a while when his wife wasn't looking. In one version of the story,[3] the father is mentioned briefly when the reader is informed that he is going away on a trip. At that time, he asked each of the three girls what present he should bring her. When Cinderella asked for a branch of a tree instead of the jewels and fine clothes requested by her sisters, he fell all over her. Is it any wonder she had problems in sex role identification, as well as masochism?

Now it happened that the King of the place proclaimed a festival to which many beautiful maidens were invited, in order that his son might choose a bride. (The Prince had difficulty in forming object relations and needed a boost from his father in order to find a wife.)

Now Cindy, somewhere in the depths of her unconscious, remembered that her own father had rescued her once upon a time. So she had a warm slosh sloshing around somewhere inside of her for him, too, plus a secret yearning that some day a resuscitated father figure would come to rescue her. (In fact, that's what she did a lot of in front of the fireplace—day dreaming that some day her Prince would come.) So when she saw that her sisters were getting prettied up to try to hook the Prince, she let it be known that she would like to go to the ball too, thus providing a magnificent target for the sisters' sadism. "A pretty spectacle you would make," they said bursting out laughing. "Go back to your cinders—they are fit company for rags."[4]

Unable to tolerate the pain of frustration, nor her violent wish to hack them to death, Cinderella withdrew from the here and now into the quiet of an inner world. She couldn't hope that her mother would "come around," remember, because a good schizophrenic mother is worse than a bad one. So she displaced her split-off needs to an innocuous fantasy mother, illuminated with a luminous halo and lit with a white light reminiscent of pleasures past. Not only that, she had a wand too. (Didn't I tell you Cindy had homosexual problems?)

Then the Miracle happened. With a tilt of her wand, the fairy godmother offered Cinderella a package deal. In one dazzling instant, Cindy was permitted to return to the womb (ride inside the pumpkin), nurse at the (pumpkin) breast, clean up in nice pretty clothes, get rid of that filthy fireplace, and compete for the (resuscitated) father figure. (Quite a neat little package. Couldn't we all use a portable fairy godmother once in a while?)

But it was only after this deprived stepchild of love had been gratified that the true miracle could come to pass. For when the godmother raised her wand again, a blinding electric shock passed through Cinderella, and she was filled with an old-new surge of love and delight. This charge of libido was able to fuse with and neutralize her remaining aggression and direct it into the socially approved drive to compete with her sisters and win for herself the Prince. The magic of love indeed had transformed her from a regressed anal character to the genital level, thus chalking up another one for Freud's libido theory.

Well, Cinderella went off to the ball with the Prince but we don't have to expound on that aspect of her psychosexual development, because Freud (Sigmund) told us long ago that almost everybody has some libido that reached the genital stage. But note that her anal fixation was evident even at this level of functioning, because in her ambivalence about returning on time, she dropped behind—a shoe! (This one had been cleaned up by the godmother, however, as it was made of glass.)

We can deduce from analysis of this behavior that Cinderella had been toilet trained too early. It appears she had complied physically with her mother's demands, but then transformed her anal stubbornness into a character trait, which became evident in her behavior whenever she was commanded to perform on schedule. Seen in this light, the act of dropping the shoe behind her clearly is an act of rebellion against the dictatorial regimentation of the domineering fairy godmother. Moreover, we can see that the power of the repetition compulsion proved even stronger than the power of love. For just as the fairy godmother first represented the all-giving mother of early infancy, now she stood glaringly revealed in the light of mother's original crime. For, horror of horrors, when the infant Cindy refused to perform, the powerful bounties of mother abruptly were yanked away. So, too, the compulsive godmother vengefully withdrew her gifts because Cindy was one instant late! You see why Freud told us the love cure will not work?

Luckily for Miss C., the Prince, like her father before him, rescued Cinderella from her anal fixation and catapulted her onto the oedipal plane. But even a resuscitated father figure has his limitations and could not completely resolve her genital distortions. Her shoe was very tiny, remember. In the opinion of the writer, Cinderella suffered from atypical ego development, in which her self image was that of a very small girl. The foot (and other body parts) of a child would look very small indeed when compared with those of her mother and grown-up sisters. Only then could she dare to expose her foot, put it in the glass slipper, and be carted off to the palace, where the Prince still lived with his father.

The writer is aware that not much data are available on the developmental history of the Prince and recommends further research in these uncharted waters. Nevertheless, careful perusal of the literature suggests that the Prince also suffered distortions in psychosexual development. Empirical data suggest he was a fetishist, who required a small foot in his love object to deny his fears of castration. The reader is reminded of his panic state and that he searched compulsively with ever-increasing desperation until he found Cinderella.

Now even though she had been disappointed in her object relations with the fairy godmother, Cindy had gained enough ego strength from her regression under the auspices of the ego to enable her to return to the genital level and marry the Prince. Let's hope they both stayed there. What about the repetition compulsion, you say? So they both went into psychoanalysis. Cinderella's analyst quickly analyzed her defenses of splitting, regression, turning anger against herself, withdrawal, and use of fantasy to deny reality, to say nothing of her oral, anal, and phallic fixations, masochistic, paranoid, and homosexual tendencies, and atypical ego development. And the Prince's analyst worked through his fetishism, homosexuality, passivity, panic states, castration anxiety, difficulty in forming object relations, and compulsive symptomatology post haste. And in due time (after they'd resolved their Oedipus complexes of course) they came to be King and Queen. And they lived happily ever after . . . at least until he said, "You'd better give me an heir in nine months . . ."

Footnotes

[1] The attention of the reader is called to the symbolic significance of the name "Cinderella."

[2] *Grimm's Fairy Tales.* H. Wolff Book Mfg. Co., New York, N.Y.

[3] *Famous Fairy Tales.* Books, Inc. New York, N.Y.

[4] *Ibid.*

A Modern Day Psychoanalytic Fable:
II. Goldi-Locks and the Three Bares

Alma H. Bond, Ph.D.
Institute for Psychoanalytic Training and Research

Once upon a time, there was a little girl named Goldi-locks. She was a pretty little child and lived very happily with her mother and father until, one night, something horrendous happened. In the deep of the night, nonplused, perhaps, by some half-felt sensation, she jolted awake. Feeling rather lonely, she wandered into her parents' bedroom, which was unlocked, of course. First, it was all dark in there, but suddenly the moon came out from under the clouds and lit up a strange apparition. It looked like two huge white animals wrestling around under the bedclothes. Goldi-locks was terrified because one monster appeared to be stabbing the other and both seemed to be moaning and writhing in pain. But, then, Goldi-locks wasn't sure, because the moans also sounded exciting. You see, she was a very curious little girl and wanted to check up on the action so that if it really was fun, she could join in. And, then, maybe she wouldn't be so scared. Besides, it is very lonely being left out of the party. . . . So she "screwed her courage to the sticking post" and called out, "Mommy? . . . Daddy? . . . Is that you? What are you . . . doing?"

Now, the Loxes usually were very nice folks, who never raised their voice to their pretty little girl. But, when they heard Goldi-locks' voice, they naturally were a bit disconcerted. Mommy yanked the bedclothes around her and shrieked "Go away!" Daddy grabbed his shorts and yelled, "Get the hell out of here or I'll beat the living nightlights out of you!" Goldi-locks was so humiliated that she let out the first recorded Primal Scream, thus making psychohistory. Then, she bolted down the stairs, out the front door, and as far away as she could.

Now we understand what Goldi-locks was doing wandering around all by her lonesome in the middle of the forest.

So, once more, once upon a time, there were three bears who lived in a lovely little house in the woods. Like all good normal American families, there was a great big daddy, a medium size mommy, and an itzy bitzy baby, only they just happened to be bears.

61

And, they had three bowls of porridge for the three of them. (Eating from the same bowl was a no-no for these individuated bears.) Naturally, the daddy bear had a great big bowl (having suffered early oral deprivation, he was a bit of a pig), the mommy bear a medium size bowl (this was before the days of women's lib), and the itzy bitzy baby bear had an itzy bitzy bowl with an itzy bitzy spoon, and well, you get the general idea. Ditto for their three chairs and three beds. Anyway, since the porridge was very, very hot, the three bears decided to take a walk in the woods while their breakfast cooled off.

After running for hours, Goldi-locks came out to the clearing in the very same woods (surprise!) where the three bears had their dear little house. "Ah," gasped the exhausted Goldi-locks, "here is a dear little house, with a dear little roof and dear little windows, and, oh boy, a dear little unlocked door! And, I'm going to go right inside! And, so she did. She really did. (As you recall, she had the habit of being intrusive.)

We'll skip the parts where she tastes the porridge, sits on the chairs, and so forth, and the bears return home and say, "Who's been eating my . . ., Who's been sitting on my . . .," et cetera, and proceed at once to the action. Where's that? In the bedroom, of course, where they all demand to know, "Who's been sleeping in my bed?" And naturally, who's the culprit but Goldi-locks, who never made it to her own parents' bed, but made up for it in the boudoir of the Three Bares. (Thus, assuring that the "return of the repressed" wins out every time.)

But, the Bares didn't like her intrusion any more than the originals of the story and, growling and barking, nearly startled Goldi-locks to death, just as her parents did 24 hours (or was it years) ago. So, she leapt out of bed, jumped out the window, and in her customary manner, ran far, far away.

And so ends the story of how Goldi-locks grew up to become a marathon runner.

3
Psychodiagnostics

Oral Sadism and the Vegetarian Personality

Glenn C. Ellenbogen, Ph.D.

A review of the clinical literature on vegetarianism to date reveals that little attention has been given to the psychodynamic mechanisms which govern the behavior of those individuals who choose to restrict their diet to foods other than dead animals. While it had been Fruit-looper's (1895) case study of Julia V., a 39-year-old pregnant hysteric unable to refrain from regurgitating Wienerschnitzels, which had first thrown light upon the meatless phenomenon, Fruitlooper's contemporaries rejected his psychosexual interpretation of Wienerschnitzels and interest in his discovery soon waned. It was not until the advent of von Krankmann, one of Fruitlooper's more brilliant students, a tireless theoretician and jogger and, later, founder of the "neo-Fruitloopian school" of psychoanalysis, that interest in vegetarianism was renewed.

The connection between vegetarianism and sadism was first highlighted in von Krankmann's (1939) seminal paper, "A treatise on the psychodynamics of the meatless choice." Von Krankmann theorized that the sole consumption of vegetables, to the exclusion of sinewy flesh, represented a "fixation" at an "oral-sadistic stage" of development.[1]

> The fixation is by the rigid cathexis of energy to but one category of objects represented.[2] While the vegetarian not so very often to other equally erogenous zones these organic substances placed observed have been, so can we say that the use of these vegetables truly, no, almost exclusively, to the oral zone placed are! Also, have we a sadistic impulse with the vegetarian character. The man who kills animals for meat gives the pursued animal a chance to escape. How more and more sadistically cruel is the non-meat eating man. The keen theoretician must himself

---

[1] I would like to thank Mr. Angelo Augratini, A.A., adjunct assistant instructor of European languages, Hempstead Community College, for his translation of this passage from von Krankmann's original text.

[2] *Translator's Note:* I kind of had some trouble translating a pretty short sentence that came after this one so I just left it out.

this question deeply ask—What is the likelihood that the tranquil carrot from its vicious predator successfully outrun can?

During his American lecture series, delivered at the New School For Social Research in the Fall of 1941, von Krankmann (1942) introduced a refinement and expansion of his work, outlining the process by which the vegetarian defends himself against conscious awareness of sadistic impulses.

The orally fixated vegetarian deals with his early prototypic loss of the love object through compensatory defense mechanisms which serve to conceal from himself, significant others, and his Saturday night dates, his deep-seated feelings of anger, hostility, hatred, rage, and, to some extent, dislike for his fellow man. Nor is his like for women too keen. Since the vegetarian character identifies man with animals (and rightfully so), he utilizes the defense mechanisms of reaction formation, denial, and sublimation in order to portray a facade whereby he is perceived as loving man, the animal, and hence animals, while displacing his true oral-sadistic impulses onto the non-man non-animal—vegetables. Thus it is that the orally-sadistic vegetarian character comes to take delight in aggressively consuming vegetables while zealously and defensively maintaining his *dis-taste* for animals.

While von Krankmann was making progressive inroads in exploring the psychodynamics of the vegetarian character, it was not until his now famous 1947 Invited Psychoanalysts Address before the faculty and candidates of the prestigious Advanced Institute For Psychoanalytic Psychotherapy that his thinking crystallized with the conceptualization of "the Vegetarian Personality." Von Krankmann's long and arduous theorizing was finally complete.

The Vegetarian Personality is characterized by ruthless acts of an oral-sadistic nature directed against vegetables. Through a series of complex and difficult (even for the analyst) to understand processes, a tripartition of the ego develops. This splitting of the ego leads to the gradual emergence of three compartmentalized senses of reality—"the good-food," "the bad-food," and "the not-food." Vegetables are perceived as "the good-food" because engaging in the consummatory act does not threaten to unleash the underlying currents of anxiety. Animals are perceived as "the bad-food" because even the thought of devouring them is threatening enough to arouse the vegetarian's fear of dealing with his repressed oral-aggressive and oral-sadistic urges toward his fellow man. And lastly, there is the primitive taboo against phylogenetic self-destruction of the species, so that man himself becomes "the not-food" and the impulse toward cannibalism is successfully defended against.

Von Krankmann's tragic and untimely death from ingestion of poisonous mushrooms deprived the psychoanalytic community of a great mind. His pioneering work in the area of oral sadism and the Vegetarian Personality, nonetheless, had an enormous impact upon the field of psychoanalysis and prompted, if not a great deal of research, or any, for that matter, at least a great deal of heated debate among psychoanalysts.

Perhaps as a fitting tribute to von Krankmann's greatness as a theoretician, clinician, and taxpayer, members of the American Psychiatric Association, in revising their outdated *Diagnostic and Statistical Manual of Mental Disorders (DSM)*, spontaneously chose, upon unanimous recommendation of the Task Force on Nomenclature and Statistics, as well as at the adamant urging of the American Psychological Association, to incorporate von Krankmann's work into their newly revised third edition, the *DSM-III*. The influence of von Krankmann's penetrating thinking is clearly evident in the passage from the *DSM-III* reproduced below.

301.85 Vegetarian Personality Disorder

The essential feature is a Personality Disorder in which there is a severe preoccupation with food consumption, schizoid-like inability to empathize with certain living organisms (usually vegetables) within the environment, hypersensitivity to issues revolving about food ingestion, paranoid suspiciousness as to the content of the dinner plate, and impaired social relationships, particularly in restaurant settings, due to rigidity in eating patterns.

Associated features. Individuals with this disorder usually are unable to express anger, hostility, or aggressiveness toward others, but fare well in expressing such feelings toward vegetables. Because of the individual's intense preoccupations with food, they commonly have impaired social relationships and oftentimes attempt to band together in social self-help groups, called "food collectives." The rigidity of their eating behavior tends to contribute to their social impairment and individuals with this disorder are frequently known to seek out partners who suffer from the same disorder.

Impairment. Eating behavior, by definition, is severely compartmentalized and rigid. Social relationships usually become impaired, as the individual gets into arguments with others over where to dine. While occupational functioning is rarely disturbed, the individual with this disorder usually brings lunch or buys a yogurt to go.

Complications. A common complication is Unintentional Substance Use Disorder, with toxicity appearing in the form of "MSG overdose" from eating too frequently in Chinese restaurants.

Predisposing factors. Finicky eating patterns in childhood may in some way be associated with the onset of this disorder in later adolescence or early adulthood, although the relationship is not clearly established.

Prevalence. This disorder seems to have become fairly common beginning in the late 1960's and continuing into the 1970's, but seems to be tapering off in the 1980's.

Sex ratio. This disorder is diagnosed about equally among men and women.

Differential diagnosis. In **Paranoid Personality Disorder** there is, by definition, pervasive and systematic mistrust of people, while the **Vegetarian Personality Disorder** involves mistrust specifically related to the content of the dinner plate. In both the **Schizoid Personality Disorder** and **Narcissistic Personality Disorder,** conspicuous absence of any ability to empathize is a primary feature, while the **Vegetarian Personality Disorder** is characterized by an individual who is capable of empathizing, at least on a superficial level, with other people and related animals.

Diagnostic Criteria for Vegetarian Personality Disorder

A. Loss of the love object early in life without subsequent resolution of at least five of the following emotions toward the love object:

(1) anger
(2) hostility
(3) rage

(4) hatred

(5) dislike

B. Onset of disorder in late adolescence or early adulthood.

C. Rigidity of eating patterns.

D. Inability to empathize with certain living organisms within the environment as indicated by:

(1) an overconcern for the feelings and physical well-being of animals (e.g., verbalizing that it is "animalistic" to eat animals)

(2) a conspicuous lack of empathy for the feelings of murdered vegetables (e.g., verbalizing, "But vegetables don't have feelings!")

E. Paranoid and hypervigilant preoccupation with the oral zone and food consumption, as manifested by at least one of the following:

(1) hypersensitivity to the issue of food ingestion

(2) paranoid suspiciousness about food content:

(a) individual thinks that there are pieces of dead animals on his plate

(b) in advanced stages of the disorder, individual suspects that there are miniscule animal by-products mixed in with his food

F. Impairment of social and interpersonal relationships as indicated by at least one of the following:

(1) decreased socializing at restaurants with friends because of the individual's arguing over where to dine

(2) need to join a social self-help group (e.g., a "food collective")

(3) exclusive socializing with individuals also diagnosed as suffering from the **Vegetarian Personality Disorder**

G. "MSG overdose" from too frequently eating in Chinese restaurants.

References

American Psychiatric Association (1980). *Diagnostic and statistical manual of mental disorders (Third Edition).* Washington, D.C.: APA.

Fruitlooper, Seymour (1895). *A case study of hysterical reactions to Schnitzels, breaded and unbreaded.* Vienna: University of Vienna Press.

von Krankmann, Ernst (1939). A treatise on the psychodynamics of the meatless choice: Carrots, celery, lettuce, tomatoes, and sundry other organic vegetable substances—You call that dinner? *J. Viennese Psychoanalytic Society, 21,* 312–384. Also in *Haus und Garten* (February), Berlin.

von Krankmann, Ernst (1942). *Introductory lectures on the psychogenesis of taste and dis-taste in the orally-sadistic vegetarian character: Theoretical food for thought.* New York: Norton & Co.

von Krankmann, Ernst (1947). Splitting of the Ego in the Vegetarian Personality: The "good-food," the "bad-food," and the "not-food." *Journal of Polymorphous Perversity, 38,* 412–437.

A Brief Report of a Psychodiagnostic System for Mental Health Clinic Patients: Parking by Diagnosis

Leon J. Schofield, Jr., Ph.D.
Clifton Springs Hospital and Clinic

Current certifying bodies are beginning to require greater patient participation in the assessment, planning, and treatment phases of psychotherapy within the mental health clinic setting. Toward this end, the author has devised a participation model of mental health, based upon a system of "parking by diagnosis." Before the patient even enters the clinic, he/she would freely select a parking space appropriate to his/her problem as he/she perceives it. All parking spaces would be marked with symbols, so that no patient would be discriminated against due to education, intelligence, or learning disability. A sampling of psychodiagnostic parking symbols is presented in Figure 1.

The author welcomes critique of this breakthrough in the delivery of mental health services in an area (i.e., the parking lot) long overlooked.

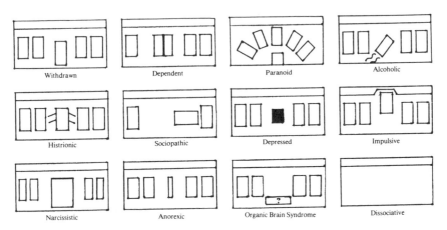

Figure 1. Psychodiagnostic Parking Symbols.

71

A Brief Report of a Psychodiagnostic System for Mental Health Clinic Patients: Diagnosis by Parking

John B. Pittenger, Ph.D.
University of Arkansas at Little Rock

In a recent issue of the *Journal of Polymorphous Perversity,* Schofield (1984) suggested that clients of mental health clinics *park by diagnosis.* Spaces in the parking lot would be marked with symbols indicating various diagnoses, thus allowing clients to park in a space appropriate to his/her problems as he/she perceives them. The author presents, here, a proposal to augment the diagnostic system through *observation of the parking behavior* of clients.

The therapist, or perhaps a full-time parking diagnostician, would observe the parking pattern of the client and note the problem indicated by the parking behavior. By inclusion of this aspect of adaptation to everyday life, we may be able to improve the accuracy of the diagnosis. Figure 1 illustrates a number of parking patterns and the diagnostic categories they indicate.

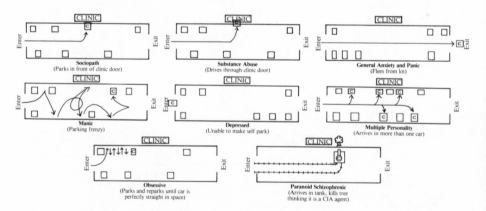

Figure 1. Psychodiagnostic Parking Patterns.

The Digital Diagnosis and Treatment Finder: It's as Easy as ABC

Kathleen M. Donald, Ph.D.

Nowadays, the busy and successful psychologist, whether working in private practice or institutional setting, has precious little time to devote to bothersome diagnostic reports, treatment plans, and psychological write-ups. For most clinicians, such activities are boring, result in terminal paperwork, demand an inordinate amount of time for reflection and evaluation, decrease the time available for more lucrative pursuits, and are, nonetheless, required. Fortunately, there is now on the market a new psychodiagnostic tool that purports to solve this clinical dilemma. The Digital Diagnosis and Treatment Finder benefits the psychologist in three ways: (1) it provides an instant diagnosis of the patient's problem, (2) it includes a layperson's description of the disorder that can be shared with the patient to facilitate his/her understanding of the problem, and (3) it indicates the most effective treatment modality to use with the problem.

The Digital Diagnosis and Treatment Finder uses a simple and straightforward procedure. To discover the correct diagnostic code, the clinician, immediately following the initial interview with the patient, digitally spins the arrow (see Figure 1) three times, recording the selected letter after each spin. (Any digit of the right or left hand may be used to spin the arrow.) Once the three-letter code has been determined, the therapist simply refers to the corresponding diagnostic label in Table 1, layperson's terms in Table 2, and treatment plan in Table 3, and speedily records this information in the patient's chart, thereby dispensing with time-consuming paperwork. As noted previously, the layperson's label, once determined, can be shared with the patient at the next therapy session. It can also be shared with colleagues at happy hour on Friday.

The Digital Diagnosis and Treatment Finder takes little time to master. Assume, for example, that as a therapist, you have spun the arrow three times, thereby achieving the following code—TBG. Employing Table 1, the TBG code generates the diagnostic label—Bipolar Schizoid Syndrome; Table 2 translates the TBG code into layperson's terms—Your Basic Uptight Son-of-a-Bitch; and Table 3 provides you with the TBG treatment plan—In Vivo Client-Centered Guidance.

Let's take a look at some more digitally selected codes for illustrative purposes.

RGM
    Diagnostic label: Substance-induced Libidinal Tendencies
    Layperson's terms: Undeniably Raving Maniac
    Treatment plan: Transactional Dream Paradigms

QSR
    Diagnostic label: Episodic Suicidal Deficit
    Layperson's terms: Bona fide Mixed-up Zombie
    Treatment plan: Experiential Neurolinguistic Modification

UJE
    Diagnostic label: Residual Hysterical Psychosis
    Layperson's terms: Garden Variety Manipulative Twit
    Treatment plan: Community-Based Vocational Counseling

As you can see, it really is as easy as ABC!

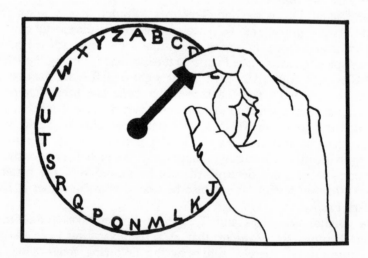

Figure 1. The Digital Diagnosis and Treatment Finder.

Table 1. Diagnostic Labels for the Digital Diagnosis and Treatment Finder.

A. Unconscious	A. Persecution	A. Disease
B. Organic	B. Schizoid	B. Disorder
C. Abnormal	C. Sociopathic	C. Reaction
D. Delusional	D. Paranormal	D. Neurosis
E. Atypical	E. Ideational	E. Psychosis
F. Post-traumatic	F. Neurological	F. Symptoms
G. Prodromal	G. Libidinal	G. Syndrome
H. Developmental	H. Body/Mind	H. Withdrawal
I. Generalized	I. Hypochondriacal	I. Characteristics
J. Psychosexual	J. Hysterical	J. Traits
K. Functional	K. Defensive	K. Fixation
L. Ego-dystonic	L. Somatoform	L. Impulse
M. Mixed	M. Autoerotic	M. Tendencies
N. Borderline	N. Hallucinogenic	N. Complex
O. Undifferentiated	O. Anxiety	O. Obsession
P. Chronic	P. Dysthymic	P. Compulsion
Q. Episodic	Q. Dissociative	Q. Fetish
R. Substance-induced	R. Paranoid	R. Deficit
S. Intermittent	S. Suicidal	S. Disturbance
T. Bipolar	T. Polyphobic	T. Inhibition
U. Residual	U. Schizophrenic	U. Dysfunction
V. Premorbid	V. Narcoleptic	V. Abreaction
W. Degenerative	W. Passive-aggressive	W. Regression
X. Acute	X. Psychosomatic	X. Personality
Y. Habitual	Y. Manic	Y. Behavior
Z. Adolescent	Z. Psychopathological	Z. Malady

Table 2. Layperson's Terms for the Diagnostic Labels of the Digital Diagnosis and Treatment Finder.

A. Pathetic	A. Crazy	A. Jerk
B. Obnoxious	B. Uptight	B. Nerd
C. Nasty	C. Guilt-Ridden	C. Wimp
D. Poor	D. Rotten	D. Psycho
E. Downright	E. Nervous	E. Twit
F. Totally	F. Boring	F. Nut
G. Awesomely	G. Raving	G. Son-of-a-Bitch
H. Goddam	H. Warped	H. Weirdo
I. Impossibly	I. Nagging	I. Bastard
J. Incredibly	J. Manipulative	J. Putz
K. Infuriatingly	K. Sick	K. Retardo
L. Terminally	L. Messed-Up	L. Ass Hole
M. Helluva	M. Sappy	M. Maniac
N. Overwhelmingly	N. Low-Life	N. Cry Baby
O. Unbelievably	O. Down-and-Out	O. Bitch
P. Certified	P. Out-of-It	P. Lame Brain
Q. Bona fide	Q. Spaced-Out	Q. Momma's Boy
R. Undeniably	R. Simple-Minded	R. Zombie
S. Major	S. Mixed-Up	S. Idiot
T. Your Basic	T. Intimidating	T. Dip Shit
U. Garden Variety	U. Complaining	U. Basket Case
V. Run-of-the-Mill	V. Brutish	V. Air Head
W. Outstandingly	W. Freaked-Out	W. Sucker
X. One-of-a-Kind	X. Over-Sexed	X. Slug
Y. Fabulously	Y. Loony	Y. Brat
Z. Friggin'	Z. Screwed-Up	Z. Noodle Head (Pastacephalic)

Table 3. Treatment Plans for the Digital Diagnosis and Treatment Finder.

A. Humanistic	A. Gestalt	A. Advice
B. Holistic	B. Client-Centered	B. Treatment
C. Behavioral	C. Freudian	C. Therapy
D. Preventive	D. Bioenergetic	D. Intervention
E. Clinical	E. Group	E. Counseling
F. Eclectic	F. Individual	F. Bibliotherapy
G. Traditional	G. Dream	G. Guidance
H. Neotraditional	H. Stimulus-Response	H. Detoxification
I. Nontraditional	I. Systems	I. Techniques
J. Interactional	J. Vocational	J. Methods
K. Classical	K. Marital	K. Modalities
L. Time-Limited	L. Existential	L. Programming
M. Long-Term	M. Milieu	M. Paradigms
N. Marathon	N. Attitudinal	N. Models
O. Experimental	O. Sexual	O. Conditioning
P. Primal	P. Didactic	P. Desensitization
Q. Experiential	Q. Autogenic	Q. Training
R. Transactional	R. Psychodynamic	R. Modification
S. Meta-	S. Neurolinguistic	S. Adjustment
T. In Vivo	T. Problem-Solving	T. Analysis
U. Community-Based	U. Crisis	U. Tasks
V. Cathartic	V. Psychic	V. Education
W. Multidisciplinary	W. Rational-Emotive	W. Contracting
X. Palliative	X. Assertiveness	X. Management
Y. Confrontational	Y. Hypnotic	Y. Contingencies
Z. Interpretive	Z. Biofeedback	Z. Regimen

Clinical Notes on "The Case of the Little Prince"

David Forbes, Ph.D.

PATIENT: Name unknown

September 7

Pt. found wandering in deserted area. Homeless, possible ex-psychiatric hospital resident. Would not give name and refused to answer questions.

Quite short, well under 5 feet but normal proportions. Difficult to estimate age. Lacking secondary sex characteristics—possible Klinefelters syndrome.

Inappropriate dress: Long scarf, '60's bell bottom pants, tousled hair, effete, flower-child-like appearance. Surprisingly well-groomed. Eyes glazed. Speech clear and orderly.

Not oriented to time, place, or person. Claims he is a prince (grandiose delusion) from "Asteroid B-612." Asked me what planet this is. Began to speak about what is "essential," or desiring what is "invisible." Distinctly paranoid ideation of wanting to get to what is really going on behind the appearance of everyday events.

Tried to engage pt. further. Showed him picture of hat. Pt. became anxious and said it was a "boa constrictor who had swallowed an elephant" (hostile, paranoid ideation). Showed pt. picture of a box. Pt. smiled and stated there was a "sheep sleeping inside." Infantile fantasy, meaning of which is unclear.

Affect: Labile, appearing depressed, withdrawn, then suddenly laughing.

Mood: Dysphoric

September 8

Pt. talked a bit more today. Revealed an overvalued notion about viewing sunsets. Expressed disappointment at not being able to see one whenever he wanted to (as if the sun literally revolves around him—ideas of reference, grandiosity). Sunset obsession could indicate melancholia. Overly concerned about a special "flower" he says he abandoned back on his planet. (Fetishistic fantasy, possibly indicating severe loss/separation from mother.)

September 9

Pt. perseverates on questions which are of interest to him—will repeat them until he receives an answer. One paranoid delusion involves a series of visits to other planets with strange "grown-ups," all of whom disappointed him each time he questioned them. (Still searching for all-knowing father figure?) Obviously afraid to grow up—almost as if he has managed to keep himself stunted so that he needn't assume adult role.

September 10

Found pt. attempting to have a "conversation" with a snake, asking it to poison him. First clear evidence of self-destructive behavior. I chased snake away. Am consulting today with Dr. von Krankmann regarding possible hospitalization procedures.

Diagnosis: Paranoid Schizophrenic (Chronic) 295.32.

A Quick-Screening Test of Mental Functions

Walter A. Kuciej, R.N.

Memory

Short-term: What have you eaten so far today?

Long-term: What did you have to eat a year ago today?

Long-run: What will you have to eat a year from now, on this date? [This question can be omitted in cases of anorexia nervosa.]

While casually covering your name tag, ask client to tell you your name. If you haven't told client your name, ask client to guess. If you can't remember your name, report to your supervisor. If your supervisor can't remember your name, look for new job.

Orientation

What is today's date, day of the week, and correct Greenwich Mean time?

Give your present location by street address, name of building, longitude, and latitude.

What is the distance in light years from where you are sitting to the constellation Orion?

Fund of Knowledge

Name all of the Fortune 500 companies.

Who won the World Series in 1883? [There was no World Series in 1883.]

Describe Einstein's Theory of Relativity in 50 words or less.

Recite from memory the recipe for Fettucine Alfredo.

On which side is bread buttered?

Mental Status

Do you hear voices? [If "yes":] Imitate them. [If client claims to *never* hear voices, refer him to audiology clinic.]

Do you ever see things that others don't see? [Note: If client lives with blind people, this can be a misleading question.]

What does the following proverb mean? A wet bird never flies at night.

[Editor's note: Earlier this year, while wading through a mass of largely uncatalogued original New England colonial period documents held in storage in the underground stacks of Lowman Library at Harvard University, a team of Harvard research historians stumbled upon a manuscript of monumental importance. The paper, written in Massachusetts in the year 1693 and published in an obscure periodical of the time, Archives of General Theology, *represents the earliest known attempt at developing a scientifically-based classification system of mental disorders—predating (and seemingly anticipating) the* DSM-III *by more than 250 years! For the first time since its discovery, the Harvard article is reproduced in its entirety below.]*

On the Differential Diagnosis and Treatment of Mental Afflictions[1,2]

Increase Mather and Cotton Mather
Harvard Theological Seminary

The presence of studies on the differential diagnosis and treatment of mental afflictions has been curiously lacking in the research literature to date. Lord (? B.C.), in his seminal study of morality and mortality, suggested several diagnostic categories and treatment strategies for those mentally afflicted but, unfortunately, failed to support his hypotheses with strong empirical data. The present study was undertaken in order to experimentally investigate methods of differentially diagnosing and treating mental afflictions.

---

[1] Funding for this research project was provided by the General Court of the Village of Salem, Massachusetts.

[2] This study was prematurely terminated due to the General Court's late adoption of a new ruling entitled *Ethical Principles in the Conduct of Research with Human Participants*. Despite the fact that the data collection had been only partially completed, the authors chose to publish their study, based on what they believed to be its great heuristic value.

Method

Subjects

Subjects (Ss) were 170 residents of the Village of Salem, Massachusetts, selected either on the basis of presenting symptomatology or suspected symptomatology.

Test Instruments

An informally prepared pamphlet, *Diagnostic and Statistical Manual of Mental Afflictions (DSM)*, was employed for the purpose of differential diagnosis. (See Appendix for diagnostic and statistical categories of the *DSM*.)

Procedure

Ss were individually hauled before a panel of three experimental judges (Es) and cross-examined as to presenting and suspected symptomatology. Spectators, randomly drawn from the Salem Village populace, were positioned within the experimental chamber in order to allow for heckling and denouncing of Ss, thereby ensuring maximum elicitation of symptomatology from the Ss. Immediately following the experimental mental status inquiry, Es assigned each S to one of two *DSM* diagnostic categories—either "295 Possessed by Satan" or "318 Not Possessed by Satan." Two experimental treatment conditions were employed—"Hang" and "Not Hang." Ss assigned to the "Possessed by Satan" diagnostic category automatically received the "Hang" treatment. Ss assigned to the "Not Possessed by Satan" category automatically received the "Not Hang" treatment. The dependent measure was the amount of symptomatology reduction experienced by the general populace as a function of the assignment of the experimental Ss to the various treatment conditions. Data were collected over a one-year period of time.

Results

A survey of the Salem Village population revealed that, while the assignment of Ss to the two treatment conditions had no statistically significant effect upon the reduction of experienced symptomatology in the general populace, the treatment conditions did result in reduction of the absolute number of members of the populace.

Table 1 shows the final distribution of Ss by *corrected* diagnosis and treatment conditions.

Table 1. Final Distribution of Ss by *Corrected* Diagnosis and Treatment Conditions.

	Not Possessed by Satan	Possessed by Satan
Not Hang	N = 157[a]	N = 0
Hang	N = 13 (Type 1 error)	N = 0

[a] These Ss were initially assigned to the "Hang" treatment, but were subsequently re-assigned to the "Not Hang" treatment following the General Court's ruling on ethical treatment of Ss.

Discussion

Our findings are difficult to interpret in light of the serious limitations imposed on the study by the premature termination of data collection. Instead of shelving our study and laying the experimental Ss to rest, we would have preferred employing a far larger number of Ss per cell. The two treatment conditions seemingly had little effect upon the symptomatology of the Salem Village population. However, the assignment of the Ss to the various treatment conditions certainly did have some overall impact upon the village population as a whole.

The failure to reach statistical significance in our project may reflect any one of several problems in research design. It is likely that our treatment conditions were of sufficient strength so as to produce a discernible outcome. It may be that our dependent variable was not sensitive enough to the effects of the treatment conditions. The most probable explanation, however, lies in the constricted range of differential diagnostic categories employed in the *DSM* itself. Perhaps a constructive replication of our experiment, utilizing an expanded taxonomy, would result in significant findings. Toward this end, two additional diagnostic categories might prove fruitful:

295.6 Satanical Possession, In Remission
296.3 Latent-Blatant Possession, Circular Type

While the research findings of our study are, at best, equivocal, several important directions for the advancement of research methodology and design were indicated, which we believe warrant the serious attention of the scientific community. Campbell (1687) outlined the concepts of "internal validity" in general, and "experimental mortality" in specific. Mather and Mather (1688), in a refinement of Campbell's work, drew the distinction between "experimental mortality" and "subject mortality." The present findings highlight the utility of Mather *et al.'s* differentiation. Subject dropout rate, or *experimental mortality,* was low in our experiment. And yet, *subject mortality* was ultimately quite high, due to the unique nature of the treatment conditions.

The introduction of an "error term" seems called for in conducting research in which "subject mortality" is a sensitive issue. We have termed this error risk a "Type 1 error" in order to emphasize the primary importance of this statistic in conducting research with human participants. The role which Type 1 error played in our own investigation can readily be seen in Table 1. Ideally, the experimenter should probably seek to keep Type 1 error as low as possible for, as our research has shown,

$$\text{Subject Mortality} = f \text{ (Type 1 error)}.$$

References

Campbell, Daniel Thadeus (1687). Threats to internal validity: Understanding the unruly dropout. In E. von Krankmann (Ed.), *"Dasteh'ichnunicharmer-Torundbinsoklugalswiezuvor" (Explorations in scientific methodology, knew and not so knew).* Vienna: University of Vienna Press.

Lord, The. *Key concepts in morality and mortality: Unleash the id? Forget it kid!* Firmament: Spectral Media, Inc., publication date unknown.

Mather, Increase, and Mather, Cotton (1688). The fine line between experimental mortality and subject mortality: N = 0 vs. S = 0. *Harvard Theological Seminary Monograph,* No. 18.

Appendix

295 Possessed by Satan

This large category includes a group of afflictions manifested by characteristic disturbances of speech, physical appearance, and church attendance. Disturbances of speech are marked by increasingly inaudible mutterings, which may lead, directly or indirectly, to the taking-ill of neighbors' pigs. Corollary physical changes include paralysis of sundry limbs and appendages, emission of vile stenches, and, in some cases, the spectral projection of one's Shape. Church attendance may be infrequent, sporadic, or, in advanced stages of the affliction, completely absent.

318 Not Possessed by Satan

This category is used when the above mental affliction is *conspicuously* absent from both presenting and suspected symptomatology.

4
Psychological Testing

Nicholas Claus: A Case Study in Psychometrics

E. M. Bard, Ph.D.
Akron Public School System

Psychological Evaluation

Name: Nicholas Christopher Claus   School: North (Pole) High
Birthdate: 12/25/?   Grade: Home Instruction
CA: ?   Date of Evaluation: 9/7/84

Reason for Referral

The client was referred for psychological study by concerned school officials. According to current observations Nicholas is overweight, laughs all the time, and often gives away all that he has. He never seems depressed but will only work about one day a year. Nicholas claims to live with little people and a deer with a glowing nose. (Cumulative records are unclear as to this student's background history.) Excessive absenteeism around the holiday season has been common.

Pre-Evaluation Impression

Post-juvenile obesity syndrome aggravated by inappropriate affect with unstable reality based episodes and avoidance behavior.

Background Information

In order to gain additional data related to social, emotional, developmental, and environmental factors, a home-school consultant (visiting teacher) was requested to conduct an interview with Nicholas at his residence. Upon arriving at the given address, the home school consultant observed walks and drives unshoveled, covered with mounds of deer feces and hoof prints. General condition of the surrounding area was hard to describe due to fresh fallen snow. The home was not lighted but the twelve car garage, located behind the main building, seemed to be aglow. The home-school consultant thus went directly to the garage area and attempted to gain entrance. He was greeted at the door by a large imposing figure and a dozen or so short subordinates. After gaining his composure, the home-school consultant requested pertinent information regarding the status of Nicholas.

It was learned that Nicholas was much older than school records would indicate and was, in fact, married and living with his wife. An undetermined number of miniature personnel and several domestic beasts also occupied the premises. Nicholas indicated he did not have much time to devote to the requested interview because the night was late and packing for an upcoming important event had to be completed. In regard to the family constellation, Nicholas noted he had no biological children but was the foster parent of over one dozen charges and cared for an untold number of youngsters. He acknowledged the unkempt condition of his property but stated, "Clean up can wait until next year." Nicholas' wife was unavailable for comment due to her involvement with various domestic tasks assigned by her husband. The presence of alcohol was suspected in view of the jovial nature displayed by the client as well as the red glowing nose of his pet deer. Nicholas, however, finally agreed to submit to psychological testing, which was rescheduled by the home-school consultant to take place the following day.

Test Behavior and Observation

Nicholas appeared for psychological assessment at the pre-assigned time attired in an unusual red and white costume with furry attachments. An endomorphic body composition was observed with weight estimated to be at approximately the 95th percentile in regard to his height and physical stature. A long flowing beard hid portions of his face, while a large black belt with a circular silver buckle was in stark contrast to his scarlet leisure suit. High black boots, thick black gloves, a long slender horse whip, and a rugged backpack were predominantly displayed (perhaps suggesting unconscious sadomasochistic involvement). Additional characteristics included a long soft red head-cover with white rabbit fur and feminine looking rouged cheeks (revealing possible sexual identity confusion). A series of brown reindeer stood positioned on the roof of the testing room. The animals made unusual "pawing" sounds throughout the examination, although the client did not appear to be distracted by this outside noise intrusion. Nicholas initially expressed mild anxiety after learning that the testing room was devoid of a fireplace or chimney but quickly regained confidence when he was seated near a large window, where he could view the fresh fallen snow.

The client attempted all items presented and frequently winked, smiled, and seemed to be overjoyed at the prospect of spreading his cheerful manner. Nicholas frequently called upon his accompanying entourage of miniature traveling companions for support and consultation, although this outside help was strongly discouraged by the examiner.

Tests Administered

Wechsler Adult Intelligence Scale—Revised (WAIS-R)
    Verbal Scale IQ: 58
    Performance Scale IQ: 185
    Full Scale IQ: 119
Wide Range Achievement Test (WRAT)
    Reading: 12.5 G.E.   92 St. Sc.   83 %ile
    Spelling: 10.6 G.E.   75 St. Sc.   79 %ile
    Arithmetic: 12.7 G.E.   95 St. Sc.   88 %ile
Bender Visual Motor Gestalt Test
Human Figure Drawing (DAP)
Incomplete Projective Sentence Completion (ISB)
The Hand Test
    ER = 8:12:0:0
    AOR = 4:4
Rorschach Psychodiagnostic Technique
Early Recollection Survey
Kinetic Family Drawing

Discussion of Resultant Data

Results of the intellectual scale indicate Nicholas is currently functioning within the high average range of cognitive ability. A discrepancy of 127 points was observed between the client's verbal and nonverbal performance. This was found to be significant at the $p = .000005$ level and suggests unequal development between the two major areas commonly associated with intellectual growth. Difficulty within the verbal realm was encountered as the examiner was only able to elicit an occasional "Ho, Ho, Ho" during formal questioning. Nicholas did not appear to take the evaluation seriously and was often laughing and touching the side of his nose while trying to give the examiner small presents from his pockets. The performance section yielded a superior profile, although this score must be viewed with caution as Nicholas commanded his miniature elves to complete the items for him "As quickly as you can." It was interesting to note that the examiner experienced great difficulty attempting to return the test items to the carrying case due to Nicholas' desire to hoard them in his large backpack. (Several attempts were necessary to retrieve the small red and white blocks, the puzzle pieces, and the cartoon pictures from the client.) Based upon Nicholas' current chronological age and overall intellectual ability, academic performance would be expected within the post-high school range.

Results of academic screening suggest Nicholas is performing around the upper secondary school level. Difficulty in written language expression was noted as the client insisted on completing his spelling dictation with gloves on while alternating red and green magic markers for letters. Math computation was compiled with a Mr. Wizard calculator, which miraculously appeared from underneath his large flowing beard. Perceptual-motor maturation was judged to be below expectancy, again due to manipulation difficulty with the large black gloves. Organization of the designs appeared primitive and immature. A smiley face with red rosy cheeks was drawn inside the circle of the first card. The fourth card was turned so that it appeared to be a Christmas tree (90° rotation) and a large star accompanied by four small squares (called presents) were near the tree. This may indicate an unrealistic fantasy association, unusual for a client of his age. The sixth and eighth cards were integrated to form a large sleigh, with the curved lines used to make runners and snow drifts.

Responses from the Incomplete Sentence stems revealed difficulty with reality based situations. The following responses were recorded: People should . . . "be kind and love one another all year"; I am afraid of . . . "nothing because I believe the good is in all mankind." These responses, paired with Nicholas' three wishes, made the examiner quite apprehensive about the subject's ability to cope with and adapt to the real world. (The client's first wish was for peace on earth, the second wish was for good will toward men, and the third wish centered around Christmas being celebrated all year long.) Results of the human figure drawing gave the impression of an effeminate identification as Nicholas drew a large (12″ high) female figure dressed in a heavy coat and large mittens. (This suggests the client may be desiring to have the elves around him for other purposes.) Heavy shading on the mittens reveal that Nicholas cannot be expected to interact in society on a full-time basis without undue anxiety over his environment. Responses from the Hand Test revealed an overwhelming interest in manual dexterity tasks performed by minority personnel. Individual card responses focused on multiple activities performed by his elves. The experience ratio and acting out ratio suggest Nicholas has internalized a high degree of tolerance for acceptance and love. The initial response time was very rapid (3″), indicating an impulsive behavior component.

Based upon the preliminary findings of the general psychoeducational battery, an intensive analysis of deep personality structure was deemed necessary and additional projective instrumentation was administered.

The Kinetic Family Drawing revealed preoccupation with domination and authority. Nicholas depicted himself as surrounded by miniature humans who were engaged in various activities purported to enhance his preconceived image of the sole provider of happiness and joy. The Rorschach materials revealed a significant amount of extensor movement, such as flying through the air, jumping down chimneys, and building doll houses. Psychotic type contamination and incongruent verbalizations were documented with regard to singing and talking to subhuman objects (reindeer) and partaking in magic sleigh rides throughout the world (delusions of grandeur). The Erlebnistypus ratio (C:M) was suggestive of external life-style aspirations. Frequent chiaroscuro (light shading) responses dealing mainly with atmospheric cloud coverage and geographic land patterns evidenced environmental compatability and rising excitement surrounding the upcoming holiday season. Color shock was recorded for several cards, suggesting internalized emotional resistance to the red determinants without the appropriate green accompaniment on a snow-white background. Form percent (F%) was unusually low (below 25%), suggesting basic reality confusion and unique personality constructs. Concern was registered regarding the abnormally high animal content (stuffed bears, reindeer, and rocking horses), and content perseveration toward toys and playful items suggested a disturbed object relationship with infantile regression patterns. A detailed analysis of Rorschach content revealed multiple items reflecting the Christmas season. Oral dependency, based on food responses (sugar plums, cookies, and spiked eggnog), was also documented.

The early recollection projective technique was attempted with nonsignificant results. The client stated he could only recall back 200 years, at which time he was engaged in the identical task of present, "Providing good will on earth." (Early childhood activities have apparently been repressed by a variety of elaborate defense mechanisms, perpetrating the denial of early activities and thus resulting in childhood amnesia.

Anxiety evoking preoedipal experiences may account for this obvious repression.)

Summary and Recommendations

Nicholas was referred for psychological evaluation due to obesity, joviality, generosity, fantasies, and lethargy. Results of this evaluation indicate an overwhelming preoccupation with happiness, kindness, and generosity accompanied by a denial of the harsh realities of the everyday world. Difficulty coping on an extended basis in the real world would be projected.

Based upon the results of this evaluation plus information obtained from the home-school consultant, the following comments are offered:

1. The assignment of one dozen miniature elves should be made to Nicholas in order to provide him with the care, guidance, and material goods with which he is accustomed.
2. Continued employment on a one day a year basis is supported as it is felt the burden to perform 365 days per year would be too taxing, physically and emotionally.
3. Direct interaction with humans should be limited until fantasy wishes for peace on earth and good will toward all men can be further explored.
4. Psychoanalysis should be initiated immediately to systematically examine the client's heavy emphasis toward the pleasure principle.
5. Dietary consultation may also be helpful in view of Nicholas' need for long term weight reduction. A liquid diet consisting solely of bubbling champagne, rum eggnog, hot Tom and Jerrys, fresh Wassail bowl and spiked punch may aid in the reduction of fat tissue (and brain cells).
6. A complete physical examination is also supported as constant nose scratching and eye twitching may be related to unknown organic factors.

The MMPI (Revised): The Midlife Maladaption Prognosis Inventory

Kathleen M. Donald, Ph.D.

The Midlife Maladaption Prognosis Inventory (MMPI) addresses the concerns of the rapidly burgeoning ranks of the over-35 crowd. Given the geriatrification of the baby-boom generation, a test of this scope will be an essential prognosticator of an incipient midlifer's capability for successful achievement of the deterioration and decrepitude of advancing decline.

Answer the following items true or false.

1. People in Geritol commercials are younger than ever.
2. Even my nose hairs are turning gray.
3. A well-dressed gentleman wears white patent leather shoes and belt with his polyester leisure suit.
4. My only remaining vice is chocolate.
5. Gravity has caught up with me.
6. My teeth get cold when I smile outside.
7. I enjoy shopping malls, supermarkets, discount stores, elevators, and the dentist's office mainly because of the music.
8. Santa Claus is a sexy-looking man.
9. Only yesterday I burned my bra and now I'm wearing support hose.
10. No one knows I'm going bald because I part my hair just above my left ear and comb it over the top.
11. Teenagers laugh at me when I dance.
12. I like pudding.
13. Lumbago is a lively South American dance.
14. The reason for my three divorces is that I'm relationship-oriented.
15. I hate Jordache.
16. I think I would look good as a red-head.
17. My teeth are okay but my gums have to come out.

18. I cancelled my subscription to the *New York Review of Books* and started getting the *Readers' Digest*.
19. I buy wrinkle cream in bulk.
20. I am a hot-blooded teenager well-camouflaged in the body of a middle-aged, graying, boring-looking frump.
21. Republicans aren't all bad.
22. My beard has so much white hair it looks like a skunk's backside.
23. Libido is a fond memory.
24. I feel out of touch with my toes.
25. "Senile dementia" is an aria from Rigoletto sung by Luciano Pavarotti.
26. The intensity and speed of sexual arousal is inversely proportional to the amount of prune juice one drinks.
27. My children are starting to wrinkle.
28. The next time I get married, I'm going to make sure it's someone my mother approves of.
29. The *Joy of Sex* was depressing.
30. I've given up the search for the ultimate multiple orgasm and am now in search of self-actualization.
31. I've given up the search for self-actualization and have gone back to religion.
32. Varicosity is the spice of life.
33. Grape: raisin:: Clearasil: Oil of Olay.
34. Kids say the darnedest things.
35. I like practical shoes.

The Minnesota Multiphasic Personality Inventory (MMPI) Revisited: 43 Years and 24 Test-Items Later[1]

Robert D. Friedberg, M.A.
California School of Professional Psychology

While Hathaway and McKinley (1943) succeeded, with the introduction of the Minnesota Multiphasic Personality Inventory (MMPI), not only in conquering the arduous frontiers of personality assessment, but in filling the coffers of The Psychological Corporation, as well, clinicians and academicians alike have come to accept as fact that the MMPI is a 566-item test. In searching through the rare documents section of the University of Minnesota Library, while blatantly disregarding personal hygiene, the author stumbled across the original text of the MMPI, only to find that 24 of the original items had been accidentally excised from the present MMPI test. It is the author's earnest hope that the presentation, below, of this lost cache will help to further the field of personality assessment, advance the author's career, and ultimately compel Stephen Spielberg to film the author's life story, with Harrison Ford in the title role.

Answer the following items true or false.

I stir fry small animals.
I believe virginity is never lost, just misplaced.
When I am feeling blue, I often have thoughts that it ain't over until the fat lady sings.
I enjoy talking to realtors.
I frequently brake for the elderly.
I water wallflowers.
I can't help but think that Bambi got what he deserved.
I cry while merging onto freeways.

---

[1] The author would like to thank Barbara A. Friedberg, Cynthia Robinson, and Linda Peterson for their help in data collection and analysis, as well as Dr. Glenn C. Ellenbogen for his editorial advice. In the spirit of scholarship, they were not given co-authorships. However, a tree was planted in each of their names in Dayton, Ohio.

I date my shadow.
Capital punishment is my favorite spectator sport.
I enjoy beating a dead horse.
I am sure a person should never yodel in public.
Librarians make me hot.
I often spit on strangers.
I believe God is my landlord.
I occasionally chase my tail.
My mother was a smurf.
I ask Moonies for money.
When I lip-read, I get ink on my mouth.
When things get tough, I floss.
I am afraid that if I think too hard, I'll get hemorrhoids.
When I was a child, my family frequently moved without telling me.
I believe a bell captain can sometimes be promoted to a bell colonel.
I think I would like the work of a prophet.

References

Hathaway, S.R., & McKinley, J.C. (1943). *Minnesota Multiphasic Personality Inventory*. New York: The Psychological Corporation.

A Rapid Screening Test for Neuropsychological Function

Robert S. Hoffman, M.D.

Purpose: Rapid screening of medical and psychiatric patients for evidence of organic mental disorder. Requires 2 minutes and pencil.

Standardization: Norms generated by administration to 50 consecutive patrons of Doggie Diner, West Geary Branch, San Francisco.

Instructions: If patient is lying down, have him/her sit up, and vice versa. Remove all distractions from the room. Ask the following questions:

1. What was the closing bid for ITT common stock at 4 P.M. on February 12th?
2. What is the world indoor speed record for the 100 yard dash performed with dog sled and 10 huskies?
3. How many times did Hughlings Jackson divorce and remarry?
4. What starring role brought Wallace Beery to national prominence?
5. What makes this test different from all other tests?
6. Who was the inventor of the Unna Boot?
7. What is the pressure per square inch of Mount St. Helens in full eruption?
8. What was Freud's comment to Fliess regarding the unconscious symbolism of pistachio nuts?
9. Which color has the lowest frequency in the light spectrum, infrared or ultraviolet? And why is this?
10. How often does a Venezuelan armadillo change his/her protective coat?
11. What is the difference between a duck?
12. Why is it hotter in the summer than in the city?
13. Name all of Rula Lenska's professional acting credits excluding television commercials.

Scoring

Number Correct	Interpretation
11–13	Mensa membership recommended
7–10	Qualified to dine with William F. Buckley
3–6	Tune T.V. set to "Bowling For Dollars"
2	Dementia
1	Anencephaly, or 100% false transmitters in cortical neurons
0	Aberrant tonsils with neoplastic change have replaced entire brainstem

The Scale of Mental Abilities Requiring Thinking Somewhat (S.M.A.R.T.S.): I. Test Construction, Normative Data, Administration, Test Items, and Scoring

Glenn C. Ellenbogen, Ph.D.

A recent study, conducted by Dr. Ernst von Krankmann and his associates at the prestigious Advanced Institute for Psychometric Research, an elite division of Princeton Test Corporation, called for the development and marketing of a new generation of intelligence tests more contemporary in content and design than those that have heretofore been known to the psychological community. The present paper represents the formal introduction of the Scale of Mental Abilities Requiring Thinking Somewhat (S.M.A.R.T.S.), the first of a new breed of intelligence measures to come out of the laboratory setting in the last quarter of the 20th century.

Test Construction

Extensive research efforts, conducted over a period of literally days and days, went into the development of the S.M.A.R.T.S. test. The cost of research and development of this test instrument, of hiring and firing scientist, purchasing pad and pencils, paying electric and gas bills, were enormous. The mind-boggling costs of test development left laboratory funds so depleted that we were unable to employ a large pool of subjects to experimentally determine reliability and validity and generate normative data. In fact, we only had enough money left over to hire one subject.

Norm's

The subject we hired to take the S.M.A.R.T.S. test was quite bright and a very nice person as well. Our subject, Norman (or Norm, as he preferred to be called), was a freshman at New York University at the beginning of our intensive and extensive testing program and, upon completion of his participation in our study, was a freshman at New York University. After carefully weighing the possible threats to internal and external validity, as well as to job security, we decided to administer the S.M.A.R.T.S. test to Norm many many times in order that we would end up with enough numbers, data, and statistics to construct at least one table. The scores, then, presented in Table 1, are really Norm's.

Table 1. Norm's.

S.M.A.R.T.S. Category	Test Scores					
	Verbal Abstractions	Arithmetic Reasoning	Visual Construction	Visual Gestalt	Visual-Verbal Abstractions	Total S.M.A.R.T.S. Score
You've Got SMARTS!!!	18-22	14	10	8-9	5-7	55-62
You've Got SMARTlets *	12-17	13	9	5-7	4	43-54
All-American Average	8-11	12	4-8	2-4	3	25-42
Room for Growth	3-7	5-11	1-3	1	1-2	7-24
Mental Vegetable	0-2	0-4	0	0	0	0-6

* SMARTlets are small SMARTS.

Instructions for Administration

The generation of a valid S.M.A.R.T.S. score requires close adherence to the same instructional guidelines as were employed in the standardization of the test instrument. Thus, test instructions should be administered exactly as they appear below.

The Scale of Mental Abilities Requiring Thinking Somewhat was designed as a *self-administered* intellectual assessment tool. When administering an assessment tool, it is important that "rapport" be established between tester and testee. Since you will be administering the test to yourself, it is crucial that you establish proper rapport with yourself. First, introduce you to yourself. Explain to yourself, slowly and in a comforting voice, the nature and purpose of the test that you will be giving to yourself today. Make sure to answer any and all questions which yourself may have about the test.

It is important, at this point, to look for signs that yourself has not become all that at-ease. Some sure signs of uneasiness are trembling, stuttering, and breaking out in hives. If you should notice such signs in yourself, try to reassure yourself that it is perfectly normal to feel somewhat nervous when taking a test such as this. You may try comforting yourself by telling yourself that yourself is not alone in feeling the way that yourself does, that many people share the very same feelings—the shortness of breath, the tenseness and queasy feeling in the stomach, and a whole variety of other feelings and sensations which appear just prior to vomiting.

You should not start the test until you have the feeling that you have successfully developed rapport with yourself and have made yourself feel relaxed and at-ease in your testing environment. *Remember: Anxiety can be a subtle thing!* Even if you think that you have succeeded in overcoming your nervousness, try to notice how yourself may be expressing anxiety to you without being aware of it. Anxiety may be expressed in the form of hostility directed toward you by yourself. For instance, you may find yourself saying to you, in an angry and nasty tone of voice, "I just want you to know I don't do well on these kinds of tests!" Again, you must reassure yourself that most people feel this way. If, after reassuring yourself again, you find yourself saying to you in the next breath, "All these tests are dumb!" and/or "What do they prove, anyway?!," you may assume with some degree of confidence that you have not been all that successful in reducing your anxiety. It would not be wise, then, for you to mention to yourself, particularly at this point in time, that on some of the tests you will be giving to yourself today, you will be timing yourself. You will only make yourself more nervous. You will have plenty of time to get yourself nervous when you get to the actual timed tests, so why begin getting yourself nervous prematurely?

Test Items

Verbal Abstractions

1. Which one of the five words below does not belong?

   car　　　　boat　　　　train　　　　bus　　　　dendrochronology

2. In what way are Cheddar cheese and Ronald Reagan alike?

3. A student always has

   A. homework
   B. spitballs
   C. marijuana
   D. zest for learning
   E. jeans

4. Which one of the five words below does not belong?

   Dramamine　　death　　neurosis　　Woody Allen　　tortilla

5. In what way are a dog and an electron microscope alike?

6. Unscramble the letters below so that they make a word. This is a timed question. You have only *5 minutes* in which to unscramble the letters. The faster you unscramble the letters the more points you earn. Record the amount of time required to completion.

   ### RRDOOIMEHH

7. Which one of the five words below does not belong?

   transistor　　penicillin　　computer　　satellite　　Pet Rock

8. As the saying goes—It was _____fit for a king.

    A. quite
    B. Roger
    C. Émile
    D. most
    E. not

9. Which one of the five words below does not belong?

    pragmatic   reactionary   utilitarian   existential   wart

10. A person who accepts in other people things that do not really bother him is known as

    A. a Californian
    B. wishy-washy
    C. an eclectic
    D. a schizophrenic
    E. a liberal

11. Which one of the following statements *best* represents the concept "concrete"?

    A. Why?
    B. How many insights can fit on the head of a pin?
    C. If no one were in a forest to hear it, would pigeon droppings hitting the forest floor make a sound?
    D. Gloria Vanderbilt jeans sell for $45.00 a pair at Macy's, but can be had for 20 percent off on Manhattan's Lower East Side.

12. In what way are an <u>apple</u> and an <u>existentialist</u> alike?

Arithmetic Reasoning

1. How much does a piece of penny candy cost?

2. How many ears does a man have?

3. How many ears does a woman have?

4. How many shoes do you wear on your feet?

5. How many pairs of shoes do you own?

6. How many shoes make up a pair?

7. John had 3 euglena and his stepmother gave him enough euglena so that he had double the number he started with. John now has

    A. as many euglena as he had before
    B. twice as many euglena as he had before
    C. three times as many euglena as he had before
    D. four times as many euglena as he had before
    E. more euglena than he can count

8. If you have 7 pennies and you lose 2 of them

    A. you would have 3 pennies left
    B. you would have 6 pennies left
    C. you would have 4 pennies left
    D. you would be the type of person who loses things easily

9. Vinnie Tortoni had 3 pennies and his mother gave him 1 American penny and 1 Canadian penny. How much money does he have altogether?

    A. 6 pennies
    B. 4.87 pennies American value
    C. 3 pennies
    D. enough pennies to buy one piece of penny candy

10. Dave had 6 marbles. His father usually gave him $1.25 allowance each week, but this week his father started giving him $1.50. With his new allowance, Dave went to the store and tried to buy 3 more marbles, but the store was closed because it was the Fourth of July weekend. Instead, Dave bought a chocolate Popsicle from the Good Humor man for 50 cents. He also lost a nickle because he had a hole in his pocket, and spent 15 cents more on a package of Kleenex tissue to wipe off the ice cream which he dripped onto his brand-new Keds sneakers so that his mother wouldn't kill him. Finally, Dave got lost but the police returned him to his parents, safe and sound. How many marbles did Dave start off with?

11. On the last day of his travels in Madagascar a man bought a used clock-radio for 1/5 of what it cost new. The man paid $5.00 for

it. The next day the clock broke and the radio short-circuited. How much money did the man really save by buying a used clock radio?

12. Tom is three years older than Jim.
   Jim is five years older than Bill.
   Bill died last week.

   Which statement is necessarily true?

   A. Tom is younger than Bill.
   B. Jim is younger than Bill.
   C. Bill is older than Tom.
   D. Bill does not care about the age differences between Tom and Jim and himself.

13. A man starts out in his car from Buffalo at 12:00 Noon and drives due south at 25 miles per hour for 2½ hours. He then turns due west and travels at 40 miles per hour for 3 hours. Finally, he turns due north and drives 13 3/10 miles before running out of gas. What good is a car without gas?

Visual Construction

Cut out the pieces below and scatter them randomly. Then, put them together as quickly as you can. This is a timed test. You have only *5 minutes* in which to put the pieces together. The faster you put the pieces together the more points you earn. Record the amount of time required to completion.

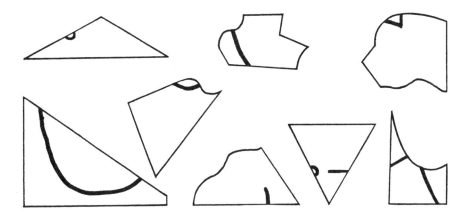

Visual Gestalt

Each picture below has something essential that is *missing*. Look at each picture, one at a time, and decide the one essential thing that is missing.

Picture 1

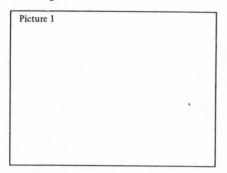

Picture 2

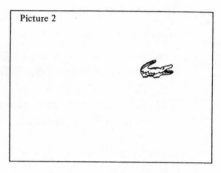

Picture 3

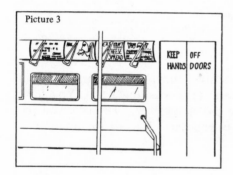

Picture 4

Visual-Verbal Abstractions

Card 1. What does this picture look like to you?

Card 2. Look at and read the card and draw on a piece of paper what you think the answer would look like.

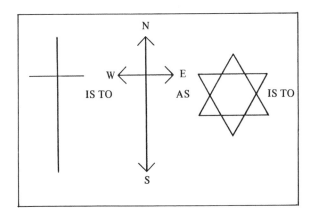

Card 3. What *one word* does this card depict?

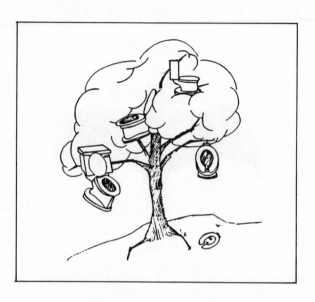

Scoring

Verbal Abstractions

1. Answer: dendrochronology
   Score: Give yourself *1 point* for the correct answer, no credit for a wrong answer.

2. Answer: they both come aged
   Score: *2 points*

3. Answer: E. jeans
   Score: *1 point*

4. Answer: tortilla
   Score: *1 point*

5. Answer: *2 points:* they're not alike
   & *1 point:* I don't know; you mean they're alike?
   Score: *0 points:* they're the same thing

6. Answer: HEMORRHOID
   Score: If you correctly unscramble the letters within
          0"— 60", you get *6 points;*
         60"—120", you get *5 points;*
      120"—180", you get *4 points;*
      180"—240", you get *3 points;*
      240"—300", you get *2 points;*
   If you were unable to unscramble the letters after 5 minutes, you get *1 point* for trying hard.
   If you gave up, you get *0 points.*

7. Answer: Pet Rock
   Score: *1 point*

8. Answer: C. Émile (pronounced "ā meal")
   Score: *2 points*

9. Answer: wart
   Score: *1 point*

10. Answer: *2 points:* E. a liberal
    &   *1 point:* either A., B., C., or D.
    Score: *0 points:* no answer

11. Answer: D. Gloria Vanderbilt jeans . . .
    Score: *1 point*

12. Answer: *2 points:* they can both be fruits
    &   *1 point:* they exist
    Score: *0 points:* they're opposites

Arithmetic Reasoning

1. Answer: any response between 2 cents and 5 cents
   Score: Give yourself *2 points* for the correct answer, no credit
            for a wrong answer.

2. Answer: 2 ears
   Score: *1 point*

3. Answer: 2 ears
   Score: *1 point*

4. Answer: 2 shoes (If the testee lives in the rural south, e.g., Miami,
            has an income below $3,400 per year, or is a "hold-out
            hippie," "0" is scored as a correct response.)
   Score: *1 point*

5. Answer: any number of pair is acceptable, but an "I don't know"
            response is not
   Score: *1 point*

6. Answer: 2 shoes
   Score: *1 point*

7. Answer: B. or E.
   Score: *1 point*

8. Answer: D.
   Score: *1 point*

9. Answer: B. or D.
   Score: *1 point*

10. Answer: 6 marbles
    Score: *1 point*

11. Answer: nothing; zero
    Score: *1 point*

12. Answer: D.
    Score: *1 point*

13. Answer: no good
    Score: *1 point*

Visual Construction

Answer: Score: *10 points:*   0"— 30"
                                  9 points: 30"— 60"
                                  7 points: 60"— 90"
                                  5 points: 90"—120"
                                  4 points: 120"—180"
                                  3 points: 180"—240"
                                  2 points: 240"—300"
                                  1 point: if you were unable to put
                                                the puzzle together, for
                                                trying
                                  0 points: if you gave up

Visual Gestalt

Picture 1. *1 point:* the picture
          0 points: nothing; I don't know

Picture 2. *2 points:* the shirt
          1 point: the alligator's shirt (a creative response)
          0 points: his shoes

Picture 3. *2 points:* the graffiti
          0 points: people, radios, crime

Picture 4. *2 points:* the sign saying "30 billion hamburgers served"
          0 points: Ronald McDonald

Picture 5. *2 points:* the words "Picture 5"
          1 point: "Have a nice (good) day"
          0 points: the soul, Psyche, pineal body, karma, lateral hypothalamus, hat

Visual-Verbal Abstractions

Card 1. *2 points:* an ink blot
        1 point: a bat, butterfly, an insect with wings
        0 points: a red ink blot, a giraffe, a giraffe with wings, the Angel of Death, the D.T.'s from the movie
        The Lost Weekend

Card 2. *2 points:*

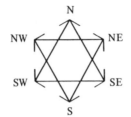

1 point:

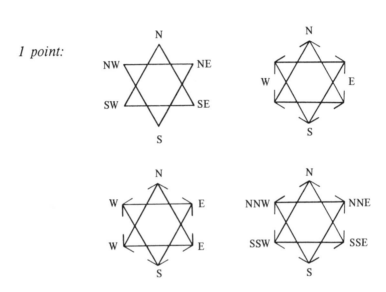

0 points:

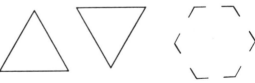

Card 3. Answer: toiletry
Score: *3 points*

5
Clinical Psychology

New Improved Delusions

Robert S. Hoffman, M.D.

As a service to mental health practitioners who are bored by the narrow range of standard delusional material presented by their patients, the following list of alternatives has been developed which may be assigned to new patients on a rotating schedule. It is hoped that utilization of this list in clinical practice will minimize the frequency of professional burn-out endemic to our field.

1. There is an evil force which steals upon me at night, removes my belly button lint, and replaces it with tapioca pudding.
2. A six-foot-five accountant forces me to floss my teeth every 20 minutes or I'll be audited.
3. My county board of supervisors has arranged for mold to grow on my pâté de fois gras in lewd patterns.
4. Members of the Kate Smith fan club, believing me to be her, are removing used Kleenex from my bathroom as mementos.
5. My Eames chair is having an affair with the Barcalounger next door.
6. Barbara Mandrell and the Mandrell Sisters are singing "special" songs which are causing excess hair growth in my nostrils.
7. Every night my ex-wife makes me drool on my pillow by beaming radioactive waves at me with her Genie garage door opener.
8. I have a special influence on the Federal government: every time I pass gas, Nancy Reagan changes her dress.
9. Hell's Angels are holding Tupperware parties under my bed.
10. The reason my hearing is impaired is that Mr. Goodwrench has installed genuine G.M. oil filters in my auditory canals.
11. A noxious substance in my Brylcreem causes my premature ejaculation.
12. Since Richard D'Oyly Carte has taken control of my stereo, I can listen to nothing but H.M.S. Pinafore.
13. No matter what I cook for dinner, it always comes out Mrs. Paul's Fish Sticks.
14. Mary Baker Eddy is forcing my doctor to overcharge me so I'll join her church.

119

15. When I try to pull one Kleenex out of the dispenser, Yuri Andropov pushes out two dozen more.
16. Yesterday the dried Wheatina in my bowl spelled out the words: "YOU ARE A NEBBISH!"
17. Marvin Hamlisch is stealing my thoughts and using them as lyrics for a musical comedy about Gary Gilmore.
18. There is a plot to turn my Rolaids into rodents which gnaw at my stomach lining.
19. I am a world-famous medical patient due to the fact that I suffer from the only reported case of quaternary syphilis, which affects only the thighs.
20. When Walter Cronkite says, "That's the way it is," he is referring to the fact that I mainline Preparation H.
21. Scientists from the Smithsonian Institute are carbon dating my undershorts.
22. Jewish matrons are breaking into my apartment to fix me up with their daughters.
23. Goodwill Industries is melting the elastics in my socks with laser beams so I'll donate them.
24. If I mix meat with dairy, Begin will have another M.I.
25. The reason my hair is frizzy is that a crazed Beverly Hills dermatologist has replaced my original hair with that of Sam Jaffe.
26. Each night while I sleep, a dybbuk in the form of Joyce Brothers enters my bed and interprets my parapraxes from the previous day.
27. My barber is actually Tom Snyder in disguise, obtaining an illicit interview.
28. People in the street think I'm a close friend of Truman Capote.
29. This isn't really my wife yelling at me; it's Ethel Merman in disguise, and she's setting my private thoughts to Jule Styne tunes.
30. When my wife says she has a headache, she really does.
31. They have altered my bathroom mirror so I just *seem* to look like Ernest Borgnine with a hangover.
32. Alien forces intent on producing an overpopulation crisis have altered my diaphragm so that, whenever I try to insert it, it springs out of the bathroom into the hallway.
33. My electric blanket is controlled by the IRS: if they can't burn me on withholding, they can fry me in bed.

34. Competing novelists are filling my typewriter keys with black goo which even sandblasting won't remove.
35. Late movies are being removed from my T.V. set and replaced with mail order ads for vegetable peelers.
36. The reason I'm always constipated is that I'm attacked on the john by alien beings with huge tubes of Perma-Seal.
37. My apartment is a mess because the Municipal Assistance Corporation is holding pajama parties there.
38. The reason I don't clean my kitchen is that I'm growing gourmet truffles in the dust balls.
39. I was not born in the usual way; I was created by Disney Studios.
40. The real reason for the Jonestown massacre is that three years ago I removed the tag from my new Beautyrest mattress.
41. The reason my new mattress is lumpy is that invaders from Venus have replaced the original springs with war-surplus latkes.
42. Every time I open my Roget's Thesaurus to find a word, I instead find obscene photographs of Milton Friedman.
43. Hodding Carter is in love with me but too proud to admit it.
44. I can't concentrate because Big Bird keeps singing to me about the number "4".
45. The reason I sound uneducated is that William F. Buckley, Jr. is stealing the larger words from my vocabulary.
46. I have discovered the Fountain of Youth, but I can't market the stuff because it comes in the form of prune juice.
47. Every time I enter a public men's room, I'm propositioned by the electric hand dryer.
48. If anyone in the United States flushes their john, I get scalded in the shower.
49. I have a third eye in the back of my head; unfortunately I can't use it because optometrists refuse to fit me with appropriate glasses.
50. R.D. Laing has publicly admitted, after reviewing my case, that madness is not in every instance advantageous.

A Brief Report on Clinical Aspects of Procrastination: Better Late than Never

Kathy Alberding, M.S.W., David Antonuccio, Ph.D., and Blake H. Tearnan, Ph.D.

V.A. Medical Center, Reno

This is a brief report of a full-length article the authors are planning to write on the topic of procrastination as a mature psychological defense. The authors have not, however, had the time to do a thorough literature review, or any, for that matter, but all have experience with the topic and fully intend to do such a review in the near future.

There are several advantages of procrastination, not the least of which is that it allows an individual the opportunity to think a task through (D'Lay, in press). When the authors actually get around to writing the article, they expect to give it the thorough, detailed treatment this topic deserves.

References

D'Lay, I. (1925). Don't rush into anything. Peoria: Turtle Publications, in press.

Acknowledgments: The authors would like to extend their appreciation to those who expressed interest in contributing to this report but who never found sufficient time to do so: Patricia Chatham, Ph.D., Stephanie Dillon, Ph.D., William Danton, Ph.D., Norman Kerbel, M.A., Kathryn McFadden, M.S., David Hutchison, M.D., Carol Vasso, and Julie Anderson.

(Received: December 3, 1975   Revised: September 12, 1986)

Burdenism

Michael J. O'Connell, Ph.D.

Being a burden to others is a skill that is widely practiced but never very directly dealt with or considered a bona fide talent. One of the main reasons for this lies in the very nature of burdenism; an individual can only fully develop as a burden if he truly believes that he is not trying to be a burden. In fact, if he becomes aware that he is not helpless, he can unwittingly cut his career short, often in the midst of his most productive years. It is for this reason that I have refrained from publishing this article for a number of years. I suggest that only those who truly feel that their best years as a burden are behind them continue reading.

For the sake of clarity I shall start off with some of the basic tenets of this movement. First and foremost is the law of conservation of energy; the concrete corollary being (in the words of H.R. Prostrate[1]) "don't choke up, soak up." I attempted to gain clarification on this statement via personal communication, but his secretary informed me that H.R. felt it would be too much trouble. Nonetheless, upon using scientific reasoning and reliance on empirical analysis, I concluded that the basic thrust of burdenism is to invest the least in an effort (no offense intended) to get the most.

The empirical base for this study is data collected from 2,542 hard core burdens. Age, socioeconomic level, race and geographic area were controlled for. There are some qualifying statements that must be inserted here. Only subjects over 18 years of age were used in the present sample. Even prior to publication I have received much harsh and, to my way of thinking, unfair criticism from many sectors, the most vocal being Y.B.A.[2] groups. In ignoring this segment of the population I am in no manner attempting to say there are not many well developed young burdens. A case in point is Z.[3] This young man was impressive and showed enormous promise. Between ages 10 and 12 he wore a neck brace to school for no apparent reason. As a result

---

[1] According to all existing records H. R. is the oldest living burden in North America.
[2] Young Burdens of America.
[3] That's his real name.

he was exempt from gym and math. If pushed in math he had a seizure. Z had two seizures on "mothers come to class day." When commanded to do a math problem on the board, the aura developed. Before the seizure was over Z had bitten two fellow students and one mother (not his) on the buttock. However, a follow-up study revealed that for all intents and purposes Z had given up burdenism by age 16. At the age of 12 his mother divorced and remarried the high school football coach. Due to identification, etc., Z gave up his liability and became a relatively mature Karate devotee. Once again, we can see the unfortunate consequences of an individual reaching his peak too soon. In general, I feel that subjects under 18 have not actually proven their reliability as burdens and therefore cannot be operationally defined as such.

The 2,542 subjects extensively interviewed were carefully screened using the "How long have you been a burden?" test and the D-A-P (Draw-A-Penis Test). The administration of the "How long have you been a burden?" test is relatively easy. The interviewer seeks out a randomly selected possible burden (i.e., unemployment records, not being in the telephone directory, etc.) and simply asks, "How long have you been a burden?" If the subject in our study did *not* respond with self-righteous indignation, he was immediately eliminated from the study. Similarly, the instructions for the D-A-P are quite straight-forward:

> I would like you to draw a penis for me. Just draw the best penis you can. Draw a whole penis and please no stick figures. Take as much time as you like.

All questions, such as "Do you want me to draw a male penis or a female penis?," are deferred back to the subject.

All subjects that produced drawings of erect penises were, of course, dropped from the study. An erect penis was operationally defined as one 45 degrees or greater using the horizontal plane. All testers were trained to not count paper rotations as erect penises.

All interviewers and testers for the study were paid and trained by ISB[4] under federal grant M-541173-Q.

The main theme of the "hard core" interviews revealed that the solid developmental foundation for success in the burden game was past injustice. Here I gained information that dispelled some long

---

[4] Institute for the Study of Burden.

standing myths concerning burdenism. I feel this new information will give hope to countless thousands who have incorrectly thought they could not hold their head as low as the next guy. The past injustice hypothesis has been well established for years (P. Millstone, 1956; J. P. Uphill, 1965; and N. Cumber, 1972). However, the present study has discovered that there is no reason why the past injustice has to be real. Well over 1/3 (42%) of our interviewed sample reported having made up past injustice stories. An even more amazing statistic was ferreted out through careful analysis of the racial factor. Twenty-five percent of the burdens that were outraged and blamed their lot in life on personal racial discrimination were white! Interestingly, all the interviewed blacks thought they were Mexican-Americans and/or American Indians.

Sexuality Survey

Stephen D. Fabick, Ed.D.
Wayne State University

1. My preferred frequency of sexual intercourse is

   a. everyday
   b. 2 to 3 times a week
   c. 2 to 3 times a month
   d. at least once in my lifetime

2. The figure to the right illustrates

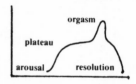

   a. the male sexual response cycle
   b. the female breast during arousal
   c. the Dow Jones Industrial Average for January

3. Vaginal lubrication is

   a. necessary every 6,000 miles
   b. only for greasers
   c. the female parallel to male erection

4. Hysterical pregnancy is

   a. "laboring" under a "missed conception"
   b. a particularly funny pregnancy
   c. false pregnancy

5. Autoeroticism is

   a. making it in a car
   b. a lube job
   c. masturbation

6. Homo sapiens is the only species which has intercourse face-to-face

   a. true
   b. false

c. both of the above
d. I don't care what those homos do

7. People who put cottage cheese in their pants

   a. excite me
   b. are Republicans
   c. are health nuts
   d. are disgusting

8. Sexual intercourse should occur within the context of

   a. marriage
   b. honesty and mutual caring
   c. the backseat of an old Chevy

9. Testicular tumescence is

   a. fun
   b. a punk rock group
   c. penile erection

10. When my mother reminded me to wear my rubbers, she meant

    a. my galoshes
    b. my prophylactics
    c. both of the above

11. Foreplay is

    a. group sex with four people
    b. a golf term
    c. a prelude to sexual intercourse

12. My favorite sexual fantasy involves

    a. visualizing my rabbi eating a banana
    b. peering at a sausage and doughnut strolling through Central Park
    c. making it with the author of a sexual survey

6
Educational Psychology and Education

An Experimental Investigation of Bad Karma and Its Relationship to the Grades of College Students: Schwartz's F.A.K.E.R. Syndrome[1,2]

Martin D. Schwartz, Ph.D.
Ohio University

It is generally accepted among professors that the primary predictors of final grades in college courses are intelligence and the amount of work the student puts into the course (Gallop, 1984), although other factors have also been identified ("Big Bucks," 1981; Dippity, 1983; Swine, 1984). These primary predictors, however, have been challenged by Shelter (1982) who, in pioneering the study of biological and immunological correlates of college Grade Point Average (GPA), found that college students with low GPAs had grandparents with shorter life spans and were themselves subject to innumerable illnesses, particularly on test days. Following up on some of Shelter's work, the author presents here an exciting new and far more complex set of factors governing GPA outcome—the Feckless Alien Karma Emission Response Syndrome—or F.A.K.E.R. Syndrome.

Method

Subjects

Subjects (Ss) were 240 college students in attendance at a large midwestern state university.

---

[1] It cannot be emphasized too strongly that Prof. David O. Friedrichs, University of Scranton, Prof. Richard H. Hedges, University of Kentucky, and Prof. William (a.k.a. Ted) E. Morris, University of Cincinnati, were of absolutely no help whatsoever in the preparation of this document, whatever they might say or claim.

[2] This study was not supported by any grant monies, despite the promises by a certain person at NIMH when he wanted something from *me!*

Procedure

With the help of a 14-year-old computer hacker, grade reports were clandestinely obtained from the records of all students in several large section classes. A team of 9 graduate teaching assistants then sorted all student GPA records into three categories: GPAs above 3.0, GPAs between 2.0 and 2.99, and GPAs less than 2.0. These groups were called, respectively, A and B students, C students, and D and F students. All raters rated all students, with an inter-item alpha of .57, which was deemed acceptable on the grounds that it would be a pain to do it over.

Unknown to either the students or the university's Human Subjects Research Committee, all excuses used by the students were then recorded throughout the academic year.

Results

In line with the findings of Shelter (1982), there were no grandparental deaths among the A and B students, a few among the C students, and a mean of 5.7 grandparental deaths among the D and F students (see Table 1). D and F students suffered from a variety of physical illnesses, which A and B students were seemingly immune to. The relationship, as expected, was completely linear.

An attempt was made to introduce the amount of work done by the students as a test factor in multiple regression analysis, but there was so little variance between the student groups (all groups hovered around the zero mark) that this was unsuccessful. Although a Pearson's r of 0.71 was obtained for the relationship between intelligence and learning, neither variable was found to have any statistical relationship at all to final course grades, and thus both were dropped from this study.

A discriminant function analysis was employed in an attempt to differentiate between the three student groups, using as independent variables a variety of clinical factors identified through Multidimensional Ocular Analysis (Magoo, 1959). This analysis resulted in a rather big eigenvalue, and an eta squared which was so large it needed only minimal adjustment through the use of Meier's Law (Meier, 1955).

Data were subjected to factor analysis, which combined all of the clinical factors identified into one big factor, which the author has previously termed the Village of the Damned Factor (Schwartz, 1983).

Table 1. Mean Number of Occurrences of Traumatic Grade Affecting Factors.

	Student Grade Point Average		
	3.0+	2.0–3.0	<2.0
Grandparental Deaths	0.00	1.30	5.70
Friends, Relatives in Accidents/Illness	0.14	0.92	6.60
Automobile Problems	0.27	1.23	11.41
Personal Illnesses	1.10	3.56	27.92
Crime Victimization	0.00	1.63	13.43
Sleep Disorders	0.00	0.20	17.91
Poltergeist Victimization	0.00	0.11	22.53
Animal Trauma	0.01	0.88	6.99
X̄ Occurrence of All F.A.K.E.R.S. Factors	0.19	1.23	13.95

Chi square= 267   df= 23   p<.0001

This factor makes it plain that students who get grades of D and F in college emit a form of bad karma which not only affects themselves, but also those around them.

The components of the Village of the Damned Factor, manifested by those students suffering from the F.A.K.E.R. Syndrome, were identified as:

A. *Inward Turning Trauma:* These students' bad karma or evil emissions are most often turned inward, causing extensive illness during the school year, in addition to a wide variety of psychosomatic complaints, of which the most common is partial amnesia (e.g., the test was Wednesday?). Narcolepsy is also extremely common, although this sometimes is merged into bouts of somnambulism.

B. *Outward Turning Trauma:* These evil emissions not only affect D and F students personally, but also those around them. Rather than the simplistic biological theory, which held that these students came from poor biological stock, which caused their grandparents to die often, it seems that F.A.K.E.R.S. students are in fact causing these deaths. Nor are grandparents the only ones who suffer. Friends and roommates of these students fall ill with great regularity and are often involved in auto accidents. Family members routinely get into "family emergencies," which require the students' presence at home, particularly on Friday afternoons.

C. *Animal Trauma:* The evil emissions emanating from these students not only affect humans, but seem to cause animals to act in strange, although patterned, ways. Cats, for example, urinate on students' notes and books just before exams, making them impossible to read, while dogs go into frenzies and tear textbooks and notebooks to shreds. Interestingly, dogs never urinate on books, and cats never tear them to shreds. This is obviously an area for extensive further research.

D. *Machine Trauma:* An extraordinary finding of this research has been the extent to which bad karma affects machinery and mechanical devices which belong to D and F students. Typewriters fall to pieces the night before papers are due, pens cease to function during exams, and both private automobiles and public transportation break down on the way to tests. This turns out to be the best statistical differentiator between A and B, and D and F students. The exact mechanism by which these evil emissions affect the workings of machinery is, however, unknown.

E. *Criminal Trauma:* It is widely known that certain persons are victims of repeat crime victimization (Cousteau, 1977), although the process by which criminals identify who these persons are has not been adequately studied. F.A.K.E.R.S. students seem to be in this group, however, as the criminal element present on all campuses seem to be drawn in some manner to steal their books just before the final examination. This process is closely related to the following *Poltergeist Trauma.*

F. *Poltergeist Trauma:* Not only are criminals drawn to F.A.K.E.R.S. students, but so are the spirit beings who play vicious tricks. These beings may act in a wide variety of manners, but evidently their favorites are to steal notes so that the student thinks the notes are lost; to jam the doors on lockers so that students are unable to get their notes and books out to study for tests; to steal completed papers from the students' book bags on the way from the dorm to class; and to repeatedly remove all copies of class syllabi from student notebooks so that F.A.K.E.R.S. students never know when assignments are due.

The poltergeists affected by F.A.K.E.R.S. students are also active outside of the dorms, making it particularly difficult for even the best intentioned F.A.K.E.R.S. student to complete assignments. Poltergeists are known to infest libraries, for example, where they remove materials essential to completion of papers, but return them quickly when non-F.A.K.E.R.S. students approach. Poltergeists completely dominate the U.S. Postal Service, which has never been known to deliver to a professor a mailed assignment of a F.A.K.E.R.S. student, although all other student assignments are rushed through quickly.

Discussion and Conclusion

The evidence from the present study strongly suggests that low grades in college are not related to the factors of intelligence, amount of study time, or amount of knowledge gained in courses. While the data presented here throw little light on what causes some students to gain grades of A, B, or C, the data do support the hypothesis that a F.A.K.E.R.S. phenomenon exists among a group of D and F students.

References

Big bucks are being made in grade sales (1981). *Fortune, 145,* 335–337.

Cousteau, Jacques (1977). Sharks inevitably attack bleeding fish. *Crime and Ichthyology Quarterly, 17,* 455–463.

Dippity, Sarah N. (1983). Grading and staircase lengths. *Journal of Educational Architecture, 14,* 135–155.

Gallop, Ata (1984). Professors polled on views. *Journal of Ontological Gerrymandering, 46,* 4–39.

Magoo, Mr. (1959). Eyeballing the data: An alternative to learning statistics. *Journal of Qualitative Research, 5,* 334–345.

Meier, Lawrence (1955). Data which do not conform to the theory must be disposed of. In *Handbook of statistics for getting published.* Washington, D.C.: American Psychological Association.

Schwartz, Martin (1983). Have our students been turned into aliens? *Journal of Alienation, 14,* 389–395.

Shelter, Tex (1982). A comparison of doctor income in selective admission vs. open admission college towns. *Journal of Medical Income, 77,* 188–192.

Swine, Ima (1984). Factors to use in calculating grades. *Sexual Harassment Today, 147,* 855–919.

The Influence of Tenure on the Productivity of Faculty in Higher Education

Edward A. Polloway, Ed.D.
Lynchburg College

References

Requests for reprints should be sent to Edward A. Polloway, Education Department, Lynchburg College, Lynchburg, VA 24501. The author acknowledges the work of D. Upper in the development of the research design used to analyze these data.

Didactosemiology: A System for Covert Communication in Lectures, Seminars, and Rounds

Robert S. Hoffman, M.D.
Stanford Medical Center

Invariable features of academic life are the continual desire of students to communicate with each other during didactic presentations, and the desire of teachers to prevent such communication. The standard methods in current use include whispering, note passing, and an assortment of facial gestures. Each has its shortcomings: whispering is easily detected by teachers and conveys information only to the adjacent student; note passing is risky because the note may be intercepted by the teacher and used as evidence in later administrative procedures; and facial gestures are limited in the amount of information conveyed. What is required is a system of covert communication which transmits information instantly to all members of the class or seminar without leaving any material evidence of such transmittal. The following system is offered with those requirements in mind. Preliminary tests have revealed that mastery of the system requires about one hour of memorization and one or two practice sessions.

Type of Foul	Signal
Boring	Rotate both fists in front of eyes
Talking too slowly, rambling	Rotate hand in circle
Moving along nicely, at correct pace	(1st down) Thrust arm forward, with hand flat and thumb up
Running overtime, beyond scheduled end of meeting	Tap wristwatch twice

Unconvincing, poorly argued point	(Incomplete pass) Wave hands across each other horizontally
Very good point, well argued or important	(Touchdown) Hands straight up in the air
Poor presentation, near total failure	(Out of game) Point thumb to door
Rigid, inflexible, can't be persuaded of good point	(Holding) Extend right fist upward, and with left hand pull it down
Unfair criticism	(Clipping) Slap hand on lateral pelvis
Personal attack	(Facemask) Pull chin down sharply
Extremely vicious personal attack	Cup hand over genitalia
Rude interruption	(Pass interference) Push both extended hands forward
Inappropriate use of jargon	Pull down nose twice
Overuse of psychoanalytic jargon	Partially close hand, and make three sharp movements of arm up and down
Unnecessary use of references	Turn imaginary page, throw book over shoulder
Bull	Shovel manure, throw it over shoulder
Use of sleazy references	Turn page, rotate journal vertically, pull out centerfold, throw it over shoulder

Confusing	Hit side of head with heel of hand
Wrong conclusion (or missed diagnosis in medicine)	Make hole with left thumb and forefinger; aim right index finger at it twice, and miss
Good news, useful information	Flip earlobes forward (like alert dog)
Bad news, useless information	Index fingers in ears, eyes closed
Very bad news	Gun to temple
Information too complex to be understood	With eyes, follow flight of information over head, to the left and rear
Lecturer is nuts	Rotate index finger around side of head
Bad digression	Move index finger laterally in wavy line
Embarrassing comment	Hold foot up in hand, open mouth
Unnecessarily arrogant	Beat chest twice with both fists
Showing off	Open trenchcoat (like flasher)
Double-entendre, covert sexual statement	Make circle with left thumb and forefinger, push right forefinger in/out twice
Very stupid statement or transparent lie	Slit throat with index finger

Do not rehire this lecturer next year	Tear up contract, throw it over shoulder
This makes me want to vomit	Put fingers to lips, blow out cheeks
I need a joint to make this bearable	Put imaginary joint to lips, inhale deeply, hold breath for 30 seconds
Time for lunch	Pat stomach twice, point thumb to door

A Comprehensive Exam for Students in Introductory Psychology

J. Randall Price, Ph.D.

History and Systems

1. Trace the history of psychology from its origins to its present day form. Mention the following people: Aristotle, Descartes, Hobbes, Locke, Berkeley, Hartley, Hume, Mesmer, Mill (both James and John Stuart), Weber, Fechner, Helmholtz, Galton, Wundt, Ebbinghaus, Cattell (both James McKeen and Raymond B.), Dewey, Titchener, Thorndike, Binet, Pavlov, Angell, Watson, Cannon, Terman, Köhler, Yerkes, Lashley, Hull, Spence, Hall, Charcot, Pierre, Erikson, Adler, Horney, Fromm, Sullivan, Jung, Murray, Allport, Rogers, Maslow, and Skinner. Do *not* mention William James or Sigmund Freud. Also, indicate psychology's social, political, economic, religious, and philosophical impact on Europe, Asia, America, and Africa. Be brief, concise, and specific.

2. Evaluate the influences, if any, of William James and Sigmund Freud on contemporary psychology.

Physiological Psychology

3. Based on your knowledge of RNA and DNA, create human life. Then, clone 40 sets of identical twins and conduct a behavioral genetics experiment that puts the nature versus nurture question to rest, once and for all.

Statistics

4. Given only a table of random numbers, prove that a random sample of parametric statistical techniques would take the form of

the normal distribution. Show the same for non-parametrics technique.

5. Demonstrate that nominal, ordinal, interval, and ratio measurements are all equal when squared and summed across columns and rows.

6. Estimate the statistical problems which might accompany the end of the world. Construct an experiment to test your theory. Use the .05 level of significance.

Cognitive Psychology

7. Sketch the development of human thought, both phylogenetically and ontonogenetically. Estimate its significance. Compare and contrast with any other kind of thought.

Research Methodology

8. Take a position for or against validity in psychological experimentation. Justify your position from the framework of general systems theory.

Practice Questions for the Psychology Licensing Exam

Adrianne Aron, Ph.D.

1. A soldier, severely wounded in Brocca's area, staggered to Wernicke's area and was later transported to a VA hospital. There, according to an orderly's report, he was seen delivering a word salad with blue cheese to Maj. Meriken Lesion, who was being treated with monoamine oxidase inhibitors for depression. The ward psychologist should first

   a. suspect the reliability of the report because the soldier's injury makes delivery of a word salad with or without blue cheese impossible.
   b. report the orderly for disorderly conduct, via memo to Gen. Paresis.
   c. take two valiums and sleep for one 90-minute cycle.
   d. alert a physician to the possibility of a toxic reaction to tryamine on the part of Meriken Lesion.

2. How many pairs of genes are shared in common by monozygotic twins reared in the same family?

   a. 23, only two of which are Gloria Vanderbilt's.
   b. depends on family SES and degree of sibling rivalry.
   c. depends on presence of T.V. commercial echolalia.
   d. the figure is unknown, but 50% were provided by one parent, 50% by the other.

3. *Decalage* refers to

   a. a process in art therapy used in the craft of psychology.
   b. decorations on block design in the WISC-R.
   c. a fetish object favored by 19th century Frenchmen.
   d. the ability demonstrated by a person who can see that sausages and balls are identical, but doesn't know how to conserve water, even during a drought.

4. Why are variables independent?

   a. they score high on the I*E Scale.
   b. O'Connor v. Donaldson assures them the right to the least restrictive treatment.
   c. they did all right during Erikson's autonomy vs. shame and doubt stage.
   d. because the experimenter says so.

5. According to Masters and Johnson, the orgasmic platform

   a. is on the mound of Venus.
   b. is used for launching sperm.
   c. bridges the moat surrounding Skinner's laboratory.
   d. is on a plateau.

6. Korsakoff's syndrome was composed

   a. before the Spanish Rhapsody.
   b. following a fugue.
   c. under the influence of Tchaikovsky.
   d. under the influence of alcohol.

7. In the mysterious memory bank robbery at the Hippo Campus of the University of Tanzania, Konrad Lorenz, Lawrence Kohlberg, and Cyril Burt, all of whom were on the premises, were prime suspects. Lorenz, who was followed into the interrogation room by 3 graylag geese and an Alsatian dog, said he was outside at the time, working. Kohlberg, who was accompanied by three conventional graduate students, said he was in the theater, looking at stages. Burt testified with a pair of twins at his side, swearing under oath that he was in the kitchen, making fudge. Who dunnit?

   a. not possible to determine; a GSR is needed.
   b. Kohlberg, but with great disequilibration.
   c. Lorenz, during a critical period.
   d. Burt, who had the audacity to publish the recipe.

8. Reciprocal inhibition is

   a. an inversion of Perls' "I do my thing and you do your thing."
   b. a form of sexual dysfunction wherein one partner's shyness influences the other's.

   c. the goal of therapy when treating manic reciprocals.

   d. an attempt to block anxiety by pre-empting it with another response.

9. "Give me librium or give me meth" is

   a. a proclamation of a patriot with a communication disorder.

   b. the motto of the Psychopharmacology Division of the APA.

   c. a request which, before it can be honored, must be submitted on a somato form.

   d. a request which, if granted, is likely to produce a simulation of an episodic affective disorder.

10. Gibson's visual cliff is

   a. in the left hemisphere.

   b. just to the north of the Masters and Johnson plateau.

   c. the place where Seligman learned helplessness and Maslow had a peak experience.

   d. accessible by the sensori-motor stage (they accept Master-charge).

11. If a test has two tails, is mean, is known to have a deviation, and has escaped from the central tendency, it is incumbent upon the researcher

   a. to invoke the principle of dangerousness.

   b. to notify appropriate authorities within 36 hours.

   c. to try to work it out with the psychologist and, if this fails, notify the APA.

   d. to train a pigeon for lethal combat.

12. MAO inhibitors

   a. are ineffective, as evidenced by Chaing Kai Shek's depression in 1949.

   b. were first investigated by the CIA, with funds reallocated from NIMH.

   c. is the generic name for Gang of Four activists.

   d. are associated with the maintenance of high levels of catecholamines in the brain, especially norepinephrine.

Final Impotence: Reasons Why I Missed the Test

Lillian M. Range, Ph.D., Morgan Banks, M.A., and Timothy Leonberger, M.S.
University of Southern Mississippi

I overslept.
I had a party on Saturday night, so I couldn't make the Tuesday test.
My goldfish died.
I had 12 other finals that day and I could only study for two.
I had to go to church.
I ran out of Thorazine and the voices told me to miss the exam.
I am God. I don't have to take this test.
It was the same time as my sex therapy.
I was in the middle of a peak experience.
My boyfriend asked me to make him a second cup of coffee.
The grocery store was out of coffee.
There was no dexadrine on the streets.
I had to study.
You see, I set my watch two hours ahead of time, so I'd be there on time, but I didn't have time to get there.
My adolescence got the best of me.
I don't have enough money to buy the book, yet.
The lights were too bright.
The naked city was getting to me.
I had to go to confession.
My mother is a paraplegic and I had to stay by the phone.
I was participating in a daytime sleep study.
My mother said it's a sin.
It was my first time and I was too scared.
The big guy on the corner might beat me up.
What final?
You never told us we had to take tests.
I thought if you had a C you didn't have to take the final.
All my BICs ran out of ink.
My bike had a flat.

My grandmother died. ("When?") 1974.
Post-traumatic stress syndrome: I got orange juice all over my notes.
I dropped my book.
I lost my book.
What book?
My dog chewed up my notes.
I didn't know we were having a test that day.
My goat had kids.
My cat had puppies.
The guy in the third row has been making passes at me.
I just got married.
I just got divorced.
The library was closed for fumigation.
I thought I dropped this course.
I am going to drop this course.
I missed two classes and I couldn't get the notes.
I forgot today was Tuesday.
I forgot this month was May.
I forgot this year was 1984.
Is this finals week?
My computer was down.
I'm too depressed.
I woke up that day with a "personal illness."
I was visiting my parents in Zimbabwe.
My herpes was acting up.
I'm a conscientious objector.
Aw, shit.
I'm here to learn, not to make good grades.
Tests are a needless tool of this competitive, capitalistic society.
Tests stifle creativity.
I was in jail.
Tests are an artificial stratification of the learning process.
I don't have to prove to you that I know it.
Who are you to test me?
I believe in other ways of evaluating students' progress.
I'd rather take a make-up.
I have agraphia and need to take the test orally.
How can tests hope to measure the innate, intrinsic worth of a human
    person?
I was in a bar.
I was in an AA meeting.

My boyfriend (mother, father, aunt, dog) forgot to remind me.
The guy in the first row has been asking me if my beard tickles.
I had to wait at home for the cable operator to install HBO.
It was my birthday.
I was locked in the bathroom.
I got lost.
I was saved.
I decided to enter a nunnery.
I just discovered I'm hermaphroditic and I'm having an identity crisis.
I just discovered my mother was a necrophiliac and I'm having an identity crisis, but it's OK because she's dead.
I just discovered my father was into bestiality, and I'm having an identity crisis.
Oh my God, I'm not having an identity crisis.
I died.
I've been here too long.

Psychology Graduate School Interviews: Tips for the Applicant

Robert D. Friedberg, M.A.
California School of Professional Psychology

Admission to graduate schools in psychology has become increasingly selective. The personal interview is a critical part of the selection process. Performing well in the interview may be the key to gaining admission to highly competitive programs. In an effort to help applicants make the most of the interview, the following guide has been prepared. The guide divides the interview into its three important parts—establishing rapport, exhibiting professional commitment, and demonstrating personal awareness. This handy guide, which can be carried to the interview for easy reference, illustrates how to impress the interviewer with charm, intelligence, and sincerity.

Establishing Rapport

First impressions are lasting! Therefore, the applicant should appear poised, professional, and warm. Putting the interviewer at ease is a super tactic. After the initial introductions, the prospective student should politely refuse a chair, promptly sit on the floor in the lotus position, and invite the interviewer to join him/her. Now that you are both comfortable, try making some small talk. A remark such as, "Hey, that Descartes fellow was a real character. Say, what are your thoughts on the mind/body duality?" is strongly recommended. Following this comment with servile flattery is a winning strategy. If you are being interviewed by a staid male professor, try a remark like, "I love your shoes. Where did you get them?"

After impressing your new friend with your obsequiousness, try acting familiar with his/her work, even if you are totally unfamiliar with the research. This will really knock him/her out. For example, the eager applicant could state, "Your work on the arousal level of the rhesus monkey cousins who marry, divorce, and then take albino pigeons as spouses fascinates me. I think it will make a great T.V. pilot."

Finally, to cement your budding relationship, praise the school's credentials (e.g., "Congratulations on the school being named the official doctoral program of the 1984 Olympics. Will Sam the Eagle be a visiting lecturer?").

Exhibiting Professional Commitment

Interviewers want to be convinced of an applicant's professional commitment, integrity, and intellectual prowess. Applicants can expect a question on their theoretical orientation. Prospective students should reply with a strong articulate response. An apt answer is, "I have always been impressed with the work of Carl Rogers, his wife Ginger, and son Roy." Typically, interviewers will try to assess an applicant's academic integrity. Throwing in a comment like, "I believe academic freedom cannot be bought but can be rented" is advised. Applicants should emphasize their motivation. Thus, the applicant should repeatedly ask if the program is hard and how much homework is required. The standard interview question, "What do you see yourself doing in ten years?" inevitably baffles applicants. Experience shows a near perfect response is, "I hope to bridge the gap between theory and practice, ease the plight of the less fortunate, and drive a Mercedes with a vanity plate reading 'HEAD DR.' " Applicants must exude intellectual promise during the interview. Liberal use of the prefix "meta-" and frequent discussions of Pre-Copernican revolution is suggested. (Note: If you are being interviewed by a California school, substitute "share," "connect," "interface," "process," and "gag me with a spoon" for discussions of the Pre-Copernican revolution.) Finally, convince the interviewer of your intellectualism by claiming your favorite hobby is aerobic reading.

Demonstrating Personal Awareness

Graduate schools are looking for students with a keen sense of personal awareness. Interviewers are interested in the depth of an applicant's insight regarding his/her thoughts, feelings, and fantasies. The applicant should agree that a professional psychologist must have a firm grasp on his/her identity by asserting, "A physician's credo is 'Physician: Heal Thyself.' I believe a psychologist's motto should be 'Psychologist: Touch and Feel Thyself.' " During some interviews, it may be necessary to substantiate your personal development. In this case, a top-notch comment is, "I am really in touch with my numerous past lives as a Grecian urn, Spartacus, and a toaster." Additionally, boasting that you can pass both the MMPI and Rorschach on the first try will really tickle the interviewer's fancy. Interviewers are also impressed with androgenous applicants. Therefore, prospective students should be sure to reject gender stereotypes. A statement like, "Boy George and Martina Navratilova are two of my favorite people" will do nicely. It is vital to only feign honest self-disclosure. Therefore, applicants should refrain from discussing participation in such activities as snorting Hamburger Helper and nude breakdancing.

Summary

Although following these tips may help bring an applicant's graduate school dreams to fruition, there are many different interviews and ways to interview. No technique will really convey the essence of your true "self." Remember: Be yourself and, if that does not seem to work out, be somebody else fast.

7
Industrial/ Organizational Psychology

A Validation Procedure for Telephone Linepersons: Implications for Sex Discrimination

Duane Dove, Ph.D.
California State College, Stanislaus

With the passage of the Civil Rights Act of 1964, radical changes began to occur in hiring practices. The establishment of the Equal Employment Opportunity Commission and the Office of Federal Contract Compliance led to legal challenges of previously accepted employment practices. It soon became apparent that employee selection procedures which excluded minority applicants on the basis of sex, race, national origin, or religion would not be tolerated in the absence of substantial evidence showing that the said minorities were less capable of performing the duties of the jobs in question.

In light of these constraints, organizations have been compelled to execute validation studies of their selection procedures. In order to justify exclusion of the groups protected by the Civil Rights Act, these validation studies must show that the selection procedures utilized accurately predict performance on the job, and that minority subjects exhibit inferior performance on the selection instruments. The present study reports the results of one such validation study involving the position of telephone lineman (hereafter referred to as "telephone lineperson"). Suggestions are made for changes in the current job structure which would eliminate the exclusion of the protected group, namely women.

The "test" used for selecting applicants for the job of lineperson was pole climbing. This task was chosen since it seemed to be an important ability in predicting success as a lineperson. The test consisted of simply counting the number of times a 40-foot pole could be climbed in an 8-hour period. All subjects in the study were subsequently assigned to jobs as linepersons and ratings of their job performance were made after 6 weeks. The results showed that not a single woman climbed as many poles as the lowest performing man. Similarly, the lowest job rating of any male was higher than the highest rating received by any female. Thus, it appears that the use of the pole climbing test is a valid instrument for selecting linepersons, *albeit* an instrument which would totally exclude women from this type of job.

Given a situation such as described above, the *Uniform Guidelines for Employee Selection* of the Federal government require that a search be made for a job design which would discriminate to a lesser degree against women. From the broader perspective of social justice, it also seems important to eradicate this bar to female employment. Therefore, an attempt was made to discover the source of the "discrimination" in the present selection procedure. Consultation with a physiological psychologist revealed the problem's source, which is purely physiological—men tend to be bowlegged,[1] while women tend to be knock-kneed. Thus, climbing cleats, placed as they are on the inside of the arch of the foot facilitate rapid climbing for men. The same placements for women result in their striking the telephone pole with their knees rather than with their climbing cleats.

Several solutions to the problem are obvious and would eliminate the advantage that men now enjoy. First, trapezoidal poles could be used for all telephone poles. This would equalize the test, and the job, in that men would be expected to spike themselves with their own cleats about as often as women would "knee" the pole. A second alternative would be to set two poles closely side-by-side. This solution also assumes that cleats would be worn on the outside of the foot. The solution would likely produce an advantage for women for obvious reasons.

A third solution would be to place all telephone lines underground. This seems in many ways to be the optimal solution. We must recognize, however, that it would require a change in our present terminology, but the sacrifice would surely be worth the gain. It is time we come to grips with the problem and ask ourselves, Would the substitution of "manhole cover" by "personhole cover" be too high a price to pay for the equality of opportunity between the sexes?

---

[1] Some have suggested that this is an environmental artifact stemming from the propensity of men to sit astride horses, etc. The present investigation, unfortunately, casts no light on this interesting hypothesis.

8
Experimental Psychology

The Issue of No-Show Subjects: A Failure to Replicate Non-Data on Non-Volunteer No-Shows

Arnie Cann, Ph.D., Lawrence Calhoun,[1] Ph.D., Ignatius Toner,[2] Ph.D., Gary Long, Ph.D., and Margaret Hagan
University of North Carolina at Charlotte

A major and important issue in experimental and non-experimental psychology is the problem of data from subjects who were not part of the study but should have been and subjects who did participate but should not have. The latter problem has recently received attention and a workable solution seems available (Spector, 1980). The problem of no-show subjects remains a thorn in the side of the dedicated researcher. Because volunteer subjects may be different from subjects who do not participate in a study, it is of major importance to determine whether subjects who do not participate in the study are in fact different from those who do.

The purpose of the present investigation was to determine if the data obtained with no-show subjects would be different from the non-data of subjects who did show.

Study I

Method

Subjects

The subjects[3] were not undergraduates enrolled in psychology classes, and all subjects did not receive extra credit for not participating. In

---

[1] Did not show.
[2] Showed up and was not at all helpful, but needed a publication.
[3] We use the old fashioned word "subjects," instead of the more fashionable word "participants," since we are dealing with people who are not there anyway, so they don't care what we call them.

order to insure the external validity of the findings, a random sample of 105 adult Americans[4] (four of them from Wisconsin) was not included. The average age was probably 25.7 years, and there were assumed to be the same number of males and females in the sample. These individuals were not assumed to be representative of subjects who have failed to show up for experiments, but since they did not show up representativeness becomes a moot issue.

Procedure

The sample was randomly divided into two experimental groups. One half of the subjects were placed into either the non-volunteer no-show category or the volunteer no-show category. The non-volunteer no shows (NVNS) were not interviewed without their permission, while the volunteer no shows (VNS) were not interviewed with their permission. The other half of the sample were designated either as non-volunteer non-no shows (NVNNS) or volunteer non-no shows (VNNS). In both cases, no data were available. Uninformed consent forms were not signed by all subjects. All subjects were then not asked to give any ratings on anything and no measures were taken. Estimates for all data were generated by three of the five experimenters. These data were then reestimated by the remaining two experimenters and reliability coefficients were then estimated.

Results

The variety of measures not taken were subjected to a multivariate analysis of variance and a discriminant analysis. Missing estimates were estimated according to a formula given by Cornish (1940). Results were inconclusive, but approached reliable non-significance, $F(3.987) = 1.01$, using Pillar's Space procedure. Because the multivariate tests approached non-significance, we felt justified in not conducting further, more detailed analyses, but this absence of results should be interpreted with caution.

Discussion

While results only approached non-significance, because we conducted complex, high powered tests that we did not really understand,

---

[4] The authors thank the population of Friendly, NJ for not participating in the study.

we felt justified in concluding that our original hypotheses and predictions were correct: subjects who do not show are reliably not different from those who do, especially if (a) subjects who do not show up at the wrong times are excluded and subjects who do show up are excluded, (b) the two samples are not compared, (c) the two samples are compared on non-data, and (d) statistical tests are not conducted or are inappropriately performed. We strongly feel, however, that some questions require further empirical non-confirmation.

The major unresolved issue is the degree to which randomly eliminating subjects who do show is appropriate. The empirical literature in psychology is replete with studies in which there are few no-shows present for testing. It is contended by the authors that this is not important but, nevertheless, justifies investigation.

Study II

In many instances, replacing the data not obtained from no show subjects can be a tedious and unrewarding process. As an alternative to this wasting of skilled, trained professionals' valuable time, we propose to develop a general multiple regression model which can provide unbiased estimates of non-data, regardless of the dependent measure employed. While this procedure is inappropriate for generating entire data sets, other procedures are available for such cases (Scott-Terry, 1942).

Method

Subjects

There were no subjects, although 37 males and 14 females inadvertently did show up for the research.

Procedure

The complexity of the procedure prevents a full discussion in the limited space available, however, copies may be obtained.[5]

---

[5] At the present time, the procedure for obtaining copies is unavailable and will probably be too complex, even when available.

Results and Discussion

The non-data were subjected to a stepwise multiple regression procedure. The final solution accounted for most of the relevant variance (See x .99). The standard errors of the beta estimates were all within acceptable limits.

The actual equation is as follows,

$$Y = a + .06(x_1) + .13(x_2) + .19(x_3) + .62(x_4)$$

where Y is any dependent variable, and a is a constant for each experimenter obtained by dividing one's age by the number of years since completion of the terminal degree. The values x_1, x_2, and x_3 are respectively the experimenter's estimates of the non-subject's IQ, age, and yearly income (averaged over 5 years as reported on form 1040 or 1040A). The values of x_4 are determined by the experimenter's rank, need for publications, and national reputation (or criminal record).

The regression equation should be used only for determining the scores of no-show subjects. Preliminary tests suggest that the estimates are inaccurate when employed to create data for the purpose of having equal numbers of subjects per condition.

Study III

While the preceding studies cast considerable light on a major research problem, other issues remained unresolved. However, the experimenters (a) lost interest and/or (b) left campus for the Christmas holidays. Therefore, Study III was not conducted. As expected, the results of this third investigation were not consistent with those obtained in Studies I and II, thus emphasizing the importance of replication.

References

Cornish, E.A. (1940). The estimation of missing values in incomplete randomized block experiments. *Annals of Eugenics, 10,* 112–118.

Scott-Terry, S. (1942). The fudge factor in the ultimate stage. *Journal of Psychic Nonreality, 3,* 3–33.

Spector, D. (1980). Induced mortality in unwanted subjects: Windsorizing the subject rather than the datum. *Journal of Nonsuicide Nonprevention, 2,* 1–2.

Recurrence of the Déjà Vu Phenomenon Among Professional Psychologists[1]

Larry Pate, Ph.D., and Warren Walker
University of Kansas

The Déjà Vu Phenomenon, or "paramnesia," is often regarded as an "illusion that one has previously had an experience that is actually new to one" (Webster's New World Dictionary, 2nd edition). However, recent replications by Agin and Agin (1977) have once again questioned the illusory nature of the déjà vu experience. Citing the earlier work of Alreddy and Siene (1919), Agin and Agin provide renewed evidence that illusions are, by their very nature, illusory and that, therefore, illusions are, by their very nature, illusory. We have all heard these arguments before, of course. In the interest of science, the present authors felt that it was time to put an end to the debate regarding the recurrence of the Déjà Vu Phenomenon. Two studies were conducted, both using samples of professional psychologists, primarily since this group has previously questioned the validity of the Faulti and Amnesis (1955) studies.

Method

This study was conducted at the Doppelganger University Psychologic Learning and Experiment (DUPLEX) facility in the twin cities, the same site used in the Agin and Agin (1977) study. The use of multiple measures of perceptions regarding déjà vu experiences enabled the authors to determine the extent to which Agin and Agin adequately replicated their own earlier work (cf. Agin & Agin, 1975, and Agin, 1976). A random sample of 1,010 professional psychologists were gathered into a large testing room and divided into four groups: (1) subjects

[1] With special thanks to the Merton twins, George and George, who provided valuable insights into the workings of the Déjà Vu Phenomenon.

claiming they had never been part of a déjà vu study; (2) subjects claiming to have known someone else who had been in a déjà vu study, but had not experienced this themselves; (3) subjects claiming to have been in déjà vu studies before and who felt sure, when entering the testing room, that they actually had been there before; and (4) subjects claiming they had never been in a déjà vu study previously and insisting they were not involved in one now.

On alternate days for two weeks, each subject, upon arrival at the testing center, was asked the same two questions by the experimenter: (1) "Have you ever done this sort of thing before?" and (2) "Is this the sort of thing you have already done?"

Results

A pairwise regression analysis of the data revealed that significant numbers of subjects in each group had, in fact, experienced the Déjà Vu Phenomenon prior to answering the second question.

The authors were surprised to find that many subjects appeared to possess prior knowledge of the questions asked (see Table 1). Roughly 94% of the subjects commented "Do we have to go through this again?," "Here we go again," or "Don't you remember what I told you last time?"

Table 1. Psychologists experiencing Déjà Vu Phenomenon prior to answering second question.

	Group					
	1	2	3	4	N	P
N	312	297	203	198	1010	
Experienced déjà vu prior to Question 2	312	297	203	198	1010	.00
Experienced déjà vu prior to second exposure to Question 1	312	297	203	198	1010	.00

This finding was identical to that of Black and White's (1955) study of paramnesis, which contrasts sharply with the colorful work of Hue and Tone (1944). This finding seems to replicate a portion of the Agin and Agin (1977) findings.

Discussion

In short, the results of this study clearly demonstrate that déjà vu experiences recur, putting an end to needless argument among the same theorists and researchers within the field.

An interesting aspect of the study for the present authors is that the conduct of the research itself presented little difficulties; we were able to anticipate each phase of the research, as if we had conducted it before. Perhaps this was partially due to the fact that the experimenters seemed to recognize several of the subjects from some prior encounter. Such an outcome could constitute a multicollinearity confound of the data, were we not convinced that the data would have been the same despite this experience. Finally, it was gratifying to find that so many of the subjects indicated a willingness to serve as subjects for a follow-up study of déjà vu experiences. As one subject indicated, "I thought you would probably want me to do this again."

Future research should examine the extent to which the Déjà Vu Phenomenon recurs in financial ("I thought I already paid this bill!"), parenting ("If I have told you once, I have told you a thousand times. . . ."), managerial ("The check is in the mail"), and dating settings ("Haven't we met before?").

It would be particularly interesting to know whether or not psychologists reading a report for the first time feel that they have already read it. This would be valuable to learn because such individuals typically purport to be in a helping profession because they were drawn to it from some previous experience. Such a study (involving multiple personalities of split brain subjects) is already underway by the authors, with some rather predictable preliminary findings.

In short, the results of the study clearly demonstrate that déjà vu experiences recur, putting an end to needless argument among the same theorists and researchers within the field.

References

Agin, H. (1976). A reconstruction of déjà vu testing methods. *Journal of Applied Psychosis,* May.

Agin, H., & Agin, L. (1975). Everything you always wanted to know about déjà vu but thought you already knew. *American Paramnesis Quarterly,* Spring.

Agin, H., & Agin, L. (1977). A review of previously reviewed reviewings. *Journal of Repetitive Research,* December.

Alreddy, T., & Siene, T. (1919). Déjà vu experiences among World War veterans. *American Abnormal Behavior,* Fall.

Black, Eve., & White, Eve. (1955). I never met a woman I've never been. *Journal of Multiple Personalities,* January.

Faulti, Z., & Amnesis, Y. (1955). Remember déjà vu? *New England Memory Quarterly,* August.

Hue, R., & Tone, D. (1944). Recent recollections on déjà vu research. *British Journal of Psychotic Research,* Winter.

Webster's new world dictionary of American language, 2nd college edition (1972). New York: World Publishing.

Psychobotany: A Budding Field of Psychological Study

Stanley Messer, Ph.D.
Rutgers University

Mickey Clampit, Ph.D.
Bentley College

In this ever-increasing age of specialization, traditional fields of knowledge have been grafted onto psychology, leading to hitherto never explored areas. We have recently seen the flowering of just such an active new research area, which some of the readers of the *Journal of Polymorphous Perversity* may be familiar with and which others have expressed a desire to learn more about. It was with this in mind that the authors undertook to write this brief exposition of a budding field emerging from the cross-fertilization of the full-grown disciplines of psychology and botany—the hybrid science of Psychobotany.

To quote from the first issue of the *American Journal of Psychobotany (AJPb),* slated for release in January 1986,

> Psychobotany is devoted to that aspect of plant behavior which can be subjected to experimental control and to standardized clinical procedures which have already proven so fruitful in the study of animal and human behavior. The task will be to unearth those variables which have their roots deep in the soil of traditional botany but whose branches encompass many of those areas long considered solely the concern of psychologists. In this way, Psychobotany has taken its place among other psychological hybrids, such as psychophysiology, psychopharmacology, and psycholinguistics.

Leafing through the first issue of *AJPb,* the authors noted articles of currant [sic] interest, including the following: "The Tumbleweed: A Study of Sturm und Drang," by the eminent Stanley Mildew, head of C.U.N.Y.'s Center for Legumological Studies. In a nutshell, Dr. Mildew deals with the apparent inability of *tumblingus alongus* S. to develop meaningful relationships to its family (*tumblingus* g.), drifting along, searching for meaning in a buzzing, blooming, whirring world of confusion. A more clinical article, "From Cucumber to Pickle: A Case Study," is presented by Swarthmore's Kenneth Gherkin, who discusses the progressively souring Weltanschauung of the American cucumber.

Marigold Buss reports on the aggressive use of the tongue in the Venus Flytrap. An interest in assessment has led Edwards to develop the *Floral Desirability Scale*. The Journal's book review section lauds Jerome Pruner, of New York's School of Applied Agri-phobic Research, for his new work, "Parallel Stages in the Growth of the Human and Vegetable Minds."

Harvard's contributions have been especially noteworthy in the pre-history of the psychobotany field, starting with the publication, in 1950, of David Riceman's *The Lonely Kraut*. A strong developmental approach was apparent in the perennial favorite, "The Weed from Birth to Maturity," by Geranium Kagan and Peat Moss. The final integration of Psychobotany into the whole of human behavior has been prepared by Professors Apricott Parsnip and Thomas Petalgrew.

The U.S. Senate has recently approved a $15 million grant for the establishment of centers for the study of Psychobotany in leading universities all over the country. Unfortunately, a jurisdictional dispute between the National Institute of Mental Health and the Department of Agriculture over who is to administer the funds has held the bill in a House committee. The President of the APbA (American Psychobotanical Association) has expressed the hope that enough money will be made available by October 31, 1985 to allow sincere researchers the opportunity to assess the personality of that patriarch of Psychobotany—The Great Pumpkin.

Cancer and Tobacco: A Bum Rat[1]

Jack L. Nasar, Ph.D.
Ohio State University

Nick Ingoglia, Ph.D.
New Jersey Medical School

We are downright tired of those anti-cigarette industry research studies which link cancer to cigarettes. In the present study, we blow smoke rings around the previous research. We establish with little doubt that tobacco is safe, but that rattiness (a characteristic common to anyone who would question our research findings) is a serious problem. This study employed dead laboratory animals and live laboratory animals to establish results. Further research is called for to examine the effects of the rat factor on a variety of other societal problems.

The present experiment was performed in response to data reported in a variety of clearly biased and misdirected governmental studies on the effects of cigarette smoking on lung cancer (Ackoff, 1968). Those studies reported high incidents of lung cancer in non-human primates forced to inhale inordinately large amounts of cigarette smoke mechanically blown into confined and restricted areas (Dedape, 1974). The flaws in this experimental approach are obvious and too numerous to be discussed here.

In contrast, the experiment described herein studied the possible link between cigarette smoking and cancer by a simple retrospective study of over 2,000 dead laboratory rats (deceased within the last 3 months) and 2,000 live rats (volunteers at major universities in the northeast). We sought to establish an important (possibly the most important) link, which has been previously overlooked (Cuff, 1978)—i.e., the percentage of dead laboratory animals who smoked during their lifetime. Such a study would allow the control not possible with human subjects and yet allow the naturalistic effects as in human studies. While this study is confined to rats, later work (if funded, please) will examine a

---

[1] While this research was supported by a grant from the Benefits to Life through Tobacco (BLT), their goals in no way influenced this research project.[2]
[2] I would like to acknowledge Dr. Mayo, a proofreader at BLT.

host of other laboratory animals, with special attention to bears in our national parks.[3]

It is the hypothesis of the present study that cancer is unrelated to tobacco usage, but related to certain personality characteristics possibly associated with smoking.

Subjects

A sample of 2,000 dead rats (DR) and an equal number of live rat volunteers (LR) were gathered from five different research laboratories of varying size, capabilities, and geographic characteristics (see sample subjects in Figure 1). The average age of the DR's was slightly older than that of the LR's. The odor of the DR's was somewhat more pronounced, as well. In fact, one Danish lab assistant was quoted as saying, "Holy #&8*#, that really stinks." These differences may have biased the results, although all experiments were performed under double nose-clamp conditions (Proboscus, 1975).

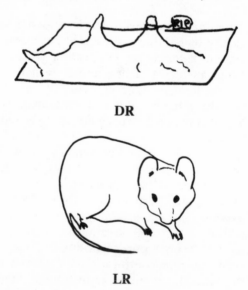

DR

LR

Figure 1. Subjects.

---

[3] It has been contended that fire, not smoke, is a major cause of their deaths (Smoky, 1978).

Procedure

The dead rats (DR) were examined for cause of death and personality profiles were drawn on each rat from laboratory personnel as well as from surviving rat peers. The researchers and rat peers who worked with each DR and each LR were asked several questions. All LR's were asked to sign an informed consent card. Dead rats were also asked to sign the card, but researchers met with little success with this group. This interesting finding will be reported in a subsequent paper (R. Mortis, 1974) by one of the lab assistants. The identities of the researchers, rat peers, and the rats were kept confidential. The specific questions asked include:

				Item Key
Did your rat smoke?	Yes	No	Only after sex	(S)

Seriously, did your rat smoke? And, yes, we really are getting paid to do this research.

Mark the letter of each adjective pair below which best describes your DR's or LR's pattern of behavior.

1. Wild	Calm		(WC)
2. Tattle Tale	Keeps a secret	Rat factor	(TK)[4]
3. Funny	Boring		(FB)
4. Loving	Hateful		(LH)
5. Mellow	Uptight		(MU)
6. Sensitive	Insensitive		(SI)

Those DR's which died of lung cancer were examined for personality characteristics noted above (WC, Rat, FB, LH, MU, and SI). All non-rats and those identified as clearly schizophrenic, neurotic, or real babies were eliminated from the sample.

Results

The results indicate no effect of smoking on DR's. The preliminary finding that, of the 2,000 LR's, many more were non-smokers ($\chi^2 =$

---

[4] No relation to Max Factor (Rubinstein, 1968).

689, p < .01), is subsequently proved spurious by the fact that among DR's, many more were also non-smokers ($\chi^2 = 6.0$, p < .01).

The cause-of-death data (reported in Table 1) suggest a rather diverse set of causes of death and cancer only accounted for less than 10% of the causes. Of those dying of cancer, certain personality characteristics proved to be salient causes.

Of the cancerous rats, 7 out of 105 were dropped as non-rats. For the remaining 98, the personality characteristics were compared. Surprisingly, there was no effect of WC (Kira, 1978). However, each other personality pair, FB ($\chi^2 = 32.4$, p < .001), LH ($\chi^2 = 71$, p < .001), MU ($\chi^2 = 40$, p < .001), SI ($\chi^2 = 48$, p < .001), and TK ($\chi^2 = 82$, p < .001) did show expected effects. In order of importance, rats dying of cancer were Hateful (H), Insensitive (I), Uptight (U), and Boring (B), in other words, real rats. These data suggest that rats with opposite characteristics, Loving (L), Sensitive (S), Mellow (M), Funny (F), and Tattlers (T), were less likely to die of cancer.

Table 1. Cause of death among rats.

Cause of Death	Number of DR's	
Guillotined	500	
Bludgeoned	400	
Drowned	400	
Crowded/stressed	306	
Cancer	105	
Drug overdose	200	
TOTAL	1911*	$\chi^2 = 421.39$, p < .01

*89 DR's were misplaced somewhere in the lab. Minnie, the lab cat, had a rather satisfied grin on her face throughout this experiment.

Discussion

While these findings may suggest a variety of future research endeavors, cheap jokes (such as, there is more than one way to skin a rat), and interpretations, it is the serious intention of these authors to point to the one clear and pressing implication of this work. We believe that this implication can best be encapsulated in one simple phrase, a lucky strike for us:

Loving Stiffs Mean Fewer Tumors

References

Ackoff, R. (1968). *On purposeful cancers.* New York: Smith Bros. Corp.

Cuff, L. (1978). *The missing link.* Tuxedo, KY: Shirt Sleeves Press.

Dedape, A. (1974). *Up in smoke.* In Cheech, W. & Chong, W. *Apes and psychology.* New York: Meade Press.

Kira, A. (1978). *The bathroom: A retrospective.* Hastings, NY: Sitting Down Press.

Mortis, R. (1974). *Dead rats tell no tails.* Rodentia, NY: Lemmings Press.

Proboscus, A. (1975). *The nose and where not to put it.* Whatawhiff, OH: Nases Press.

Rubinstein, H. (1968). *The Max Factor.* Hollywood, CA: Vanity Press.

Smoky, T.B. (1978). Only you can prevent forest fires. *Journal of Fire Prevention, 8(1),* 412–415.

Recurrence of the Déjà Vu Phenomenon Among Professional Psychologists[1]

Larry Pate, Ph.D., and Warren Walker
University of Kansas

The Déjà Vu Phenomenon, or "paramnesia," is often regarded as an "illusion that one has previously had an experience that is actually new to one" (Webster's New World Dictionary, 2nd edition). However, recent replications by Agin and Agin (1977) have once again questioned the illusory nature of the déjà vu experience. Citing the earlier work of Alreddy and Siene (1919), Agin and Agin provide renewed evidence that illusions are, by their very nature, illusory and that, therefore, illusions are, by their very nature, illusory. We have all heard these arguments before, of course. In the interest of science, the present authors felt that it was time to put an end to the debate regarding the recurrence of the Déjà Vu Phenomenon. Two studies were conducted, both using samples of professional psychologists, primarily since this group has previously questioned the validity of the Faulti and Amnesis (1955) studies.

Method

This study was conducted at the Doppelganger University Psychologic Learning and Experiment (DUPLEX) facility in the twin cities, the same site used in the Agin and Agin (1977) study. The use of multiple measures of perceptions regarding déjà vu experiences enabled the authors to determine the extent to which Agin and Agin adequately replicated their own earlier work (cf. Agin & Agin, 1975, and Agin, 1976). A random sample of 1,010 professional psychologists were gathered into a large testing room and divided into four groups: (1) subjects

---

[1] With special thanks to the Merton twins, George and George, who provided valuable insights into the workings of the Déjà Vu Phenomenon.

174

claiming they had never been part of a déjà vu study; (2) subjects claiming to have known someone else who had been in a déjà vu study, but had not experienced this themselves; (3) subjects claiming to have been in déjà vu studies before and who felt sure, when entering the testing room, that they actually had been there before; and (4) subjects claiming they had never been in a déjà vu study previously and insisting they were not involved in one now.

On alternate days for two weeks, each subject, upon arrival at the testing center, was asked the same two questions by the experimenter: (1) "Have you ever done this sort of thing before?" and (2) "Is this the sort of thing you have already done?"

Results

A pairwise regression analysis of the data revealed that significant numbers of subjects in each group had, in fact, experienced the Déjà Vu Phenomenon prior to answering the second question.

The authors were surprised to find that many subjects appeared to possess prior knowledge of the questions asked (see Table 1). Roughly 94% of the subjects commented "Do we have to go through this again?," "Here we go again," or "Don't you remember what I told you last time?"

Table 1. Psychologists experiencing Déjà Vu Phenomenon prior to answering second question.

| | Group | | | | | |
	1	2	3	4	$\underline{N}$	P
$\underline{N}$	312	297	203	198	1010	
Experienced déjà vu prior to Question 2	312	297	203	198	1010	.00
Experienced déjà vu prior to second exposure to Question 1	312	297	203	198	1010	.00

This finding was identical to that of Black and White's (1955) study of paramnesis, which contrasts sharply with the colorful work of Hue and Tone (1944). This finding seems to replicate a portion of the Agin and Agin (1977) findings.

Discussion

In short, the results of this study clearly demonstrate that déjà vu experiences recur, putting an end to needless argument among the same theorists and researchers within the field.

An interesting aspect of the study for the present authors is that the conduct of the research itself presented little difficulties; we were able to anticipate each phase of the research, as if we had conducted it before. Perhaps this was partially due to the fact that the experimenters seemed to recognize several of the subjects from some prior encounter. Such an outcome could constitute a multicollinearity confound of the data, were we not convinced that the data would have been the same despite this experience. Finally, it was gratifying to find that so many of the subjects indicated a willingness to serve as subjects for a follow-up study of déjà vu experiences. As one subject indicated, "I thought you would probably want me to do this again."

Future research should examine the extent to which the Déjà Vu Phenomenon recurs in financial ("I thought I already paid this bill!"), parenting ("If I have told you once, I have told you a thousand times. . . ."), managerial ("The check is in the mail"), and dating settings ("Haven't we met before?").

It would be particularly interesting to know whether or not psychologists reading a report for the first time feel that they have already read it. This would be valuable to learn because such individuals typically purport to be in a helping profession because they were drawn to it from some previous experience. Such a study (involving multiple personalities of split brain subjects) is already underway by the authors, with some rather predictable preliminary findings.

In short, the results of the study clearly demonstrate that déjà vu experiences recur, putting an end to needless argument among the same theorists and researchers within the field.

References

Agin, H. (1976). A reconstruction of déjà vu testing methods. *Journal of Applied Psychosis,* May.

Agin, H., & Agin, L. (1975). Everything you always wanted to know about déjà vu but thought you already knew. *American Paramnesis Quarterly,* Spring.

Agin, H., & Agin, L. (1977). A review of previously reviewed reviewings. *Journal of Repetitive Research,* December.

Alreddy, T., & Siene, T. (1919). Déjà vu experiences among World War veterans. *American Abnormal Behavior,* Fall.

Black, Eve., & White, Eve. (1955). I never met a woman I've never been. *Journal of Multiple Personalities,* January.

Faulti, Z., & Amnesis, Y. (1955). Remember déjà vu? *New England Memory Quarterly,* August.

Hue, R., & Tone, D. (1944). Recent recollections on déjà vu research. *British Journal of Psychotic Research,* Winter.

Webster's new world dictionary of American language, 2nd college edition (1972). New York: World Publishing.

9
Developmental/ Child Psychology

Toys for Tots: Recommendations by Psychological Experts

W. Scott Terry, Ph.D., Lawrence G. Calhoun, Ph.D., and Arnie Cann, Ph.D.
University of North Carolina at Charlotte

Being psychologists is not easy. We are frequently asked by parents for recommendations for children's toys. Fortunately, our training has prepared us to recognize those qualities in toys that make them developmentally enlightening, as well as entertaining. While it can be helpful for psychologists to recommend toys that are already available, the most useful approach (based on the general concept of prevention, currently very popular in community psychology circles) is to eliminate the middleperson and develop our own toys. After careful study and years of training (not necessarily in that order), we have developed a list of toys that *need* to be manufactured. These are toys derived from years of painstaking research by respected psychologists. All toys have been laboratory tested for parents' peace of mind, will improve the child's psychological development, and will enhance, or at least influence, the development of psychologists (if a large toy manufacturer likes this article).

Little Albert Phobia Kit

The kit contains a soft, cuddly, cute little doll (anatomically incorrect so as to not anger members of the moral minority) named Albert, and a matched pair of diesel air horns color-coordinated with Albert's outfit. Step-by-step instructions will tell your child how to condition his or her friends, playmates, or younger siblings, who are encouraged to hug Albert, while your junior psychologist (child-sized white lab coat can be purchased separately) blasts them with noise bursts from the air horns. Not only will these other kids leave Albert alone but they, with time, develop generalized phobic reactions to other dolls and small furry adults. For an extra $35.00, a mother-in-law adaptation unit can be added to the phobia kit.

Penfield Self-Stimulator

This incomparable toy comes with an electrical brain stimulator unit, a color-coded map of "brain parts," one set of bipolar depth electrodes, and all wires (batteries not included—use of saw, hammer, and screwdriver needed for proper operation). This kit will enable the child to implant electrodes, choose brain sites (adult supervision suggested on site selection), and do self-stimulation experiments. Gives firsthand experience in Penfield's famous demonstrations: doubling-of-consciousness, epileptic auras, involuntary movements, and activation of remote memories. Great for those cold winter days when school may be closed because of holidays or blizzards. Note that an optional stereotaxis unit is available.

Kluver-Bucey Syndrome Kit

Provides endless hours of entertainment following bilateral lesions of the temporal lobes. This is especially recommended for children who are picky eaters (they will now eat anything placed before them, food or not) or for those with repressed id desires (the child will be truly polymorphously perverse!). This kit may be particularly useful to parents who want to coax a child into a medical career. For this purpose, it is recommended for use only on other children or pets. A set of APA guidelines for research with family pets is included in all kits.

20-in-1 Perceptual Distortion Kit

Transfer your whole house into a visual illusion! Doors become Müller-Lyers; rooms become Necker cubes; stairs become impossible figures, recursing infinitely on themselves! Also includes inverted-lens goggles for perceptual readaptation experiences, and 3-D wall posters with red lens glasses. Comes complete with instructions written on color blindness patterns. Also available in a perceptual distortion party kit useful for helping up to 20 shy persons to mingle. The kit also comes in handy for encouraging out-of-town guests to leave for home.

Sensory Deprivation Tank

Comes in several sizes, from small child to obese adult. All tanks are portable and easy to use. Set yourself floating in this light-proof, sound-proof chamber. Includes a timer that can be set for 24-72 hours. Ideal for use as a "time-out" location when disciplining your child. Also available in a nonfloating model, which can be loaned to persons of your choice.

Bystander Apathy Game

This is just like the "real world!" The kit includes a decision tree that helps the child develop a variety of convincing excuses for ignoring others' cries for help, a button that says, "Born in New Jersey," and a genuine New York City subway token. The game can be played indoors (the pure science version) or anywhere there are "real" people (the applied version). Children are encouraged to go anywhere another person may need help and then not give any. The advanced version teaches the child how to encourage apathy in others. A special addition can be purchased separately that is adapted to television news. The addition covers poverty, world hunger, crime, the Reagan administration, war, and local government (special supplements will be sent if you are on the mailing list).

Visual Cliff Playard

You can have hours of fun with your crawling infant in this brightly colored play area. The step-like structure is painted in a checkerboard pattern (available in six color schemes), and includes a Plexiglas panel which can be removed to create *real cliffs*. Ideal for training your child not to trust visual information. Can be bought at a discount if purchased together with the *Bystander Apathy Game.*

Faces of Eve Imaginary Friends Kit

Teaches your child to express his or her own personality while an alternative personality emerges. With practice, as many as nine personalities can be created. Step-by-step instructions allow even the well-adjusted child to develop abnormal personalities. The child can have a whole set of friends to play with without the bother of actual children! This kit is highly recommended for the only child.

Future Directions

We hope this list proves helpful, especially to child psychologists. We are currently developing a line of toys for adults that will include *The Shyness Game* (designed for solo players), *The Social Psychology Obedience Game* (you'd better try it), and *"Let's Vote to See If It Really Is a Disease" Psychiatric Nomenclature Game* (available only to persons with medical degrees).

Perceptual Preferences in *Homo Professoria:* No News Is Bad News

R. E. M. Kleinberg
William Proxmire Laboratory of Phrenology and Introspection
Madison, Wisconsin

Fantz (1961) reported that infants prefer to look at a drawing of a face rather than newsprint (see Figure 1). His results have since been replicated enough times to rule out the alternative hypothesis that he fudged his data. The present study was aimed at reporting whether the preference-for-faces-over-newsprint effect is stable over the adult years, or any other publishable finding.

Interesting   Boring

Figure 1. Preference stimuli presented in the study of Fantz (1961).

Method

Subjects

Five "typical" male subjects were carefully selected in order to ensure generalizability of results. Subjects were employed at the author's former university and held such titles as "assistant professor" and "department chairman." At the time of data collection, all subjects were married. Subject ages ranged from 26 years, 2 months, to 51 years, 8 months, with a mean of 36 years, 1 month. Subjects did not know they were subjects (see exception, below), so no ethical problems were encountered. All subjects, henceforth called "participants," subscribed to an evening newspaper.

185

Procedure

Participants' wives were confidentially interviewed in their homes regarding the participants' visual behavior between the hours of 5 and 6 P.M. weekdays. The interviewer, a tall, male Caucasian, maintained a sympathetic but objective attitude at all times. By the method of Calculated Intuition developed by the author (available to those researchers willing to attend the author's workshop for a nominal fee), each participant was assigned a score from 3 to 17, according to their preference for facial stimuli versus newsprint during the designated hour. In the interest of reliability, a time series analysis was attempted by utilizing repeated measures with the spouse of one participant but was, unfortunately, discontinued upon the discovery by said participant and, despite considerable debriefing, the onset of incompatible affective behavior.

Results and Discussion

Data were analyzed according to a method called "groking" (McAdam & Rebert, 1977) or "looking at the data." Results almost unambiguously suggested that all participants preferred newsprint over facial stimuli. However, a linear trend for age indicated the preference was particularly apparent in older subjects. Post hoc data-picking yielded the additional finding that the preference did not generalize to other forms of print, especially books, except for younger participants without tenure.

The present results indicate a clear reversal by adults of the alleged preference for faces over newsprint reported by infants. Subsequent research conducted by the author at his new institution suggests the adult preference for newsprint may not be manifested when comparison stimuli are provided by department secretaries rather than faculty wives. Such preferences, however, seem to interact complexly with physiognomic and anatomical variables.

References

Fantz, R.L. (1961). The origin of form perception. *Scientific American, 204,* 66–72.

McAdam, D.W., & Rebert, C.S. (1977). Grok: A sidestep in the development of statistics for variance independent data. *Journal of Irreproducible Results, 23*(1), 3.

10
Statistics

Mode to Stats

Amy Katz

Anova great X bar; I was there last summa. For a binomial fee you get some great formulas (there's homogeneous milk for the total squares!). The 'cheffe is rather conservative, but occasionally he experiments. Once, I sampled a prime t steak and eta Tukey with stuffing. The leg of lambda is even beta.

Although some standard deviants correlate there, the matrix d' takes care of them. Generally, it's a good place for interaction with "chi"s. They arrive at continuous intervals and I've had several datas. Of course, I've been falsely rejected a number of times and it's affected my confidence level. After matching, people go to Hotelling's and score (never three way, nicely curvylinear). Occasionally, replication results, depending on your degree of freedom.

Well, that's null there is. Don't look for any grand meanings. The simple main effect is hopefully a*mu*sement!

A Statistically Significant Dinner at the Hotelling Vancouver

The Right Reverend Canonical Correlation will say grace at .05 precisely.

A Priori
(served on the path analysis by the pooled variance)

Two sample canapés
Split-plot and beta bits soup
Latent roots and vegetables

1st Principal Components

Cochran & Mussels
Herring Rho on a matrix of Busted Factorials
Fisher & Chips

Main Effect

Pheasant under Glass & Stanley
Roast Tukey & Bayes Leaf Dressing
Bonferroni (the San Francisco treat) with Anastasi Sauce
Roast Suckling Pig rotated obliquely over charcoal
Wilk's Lambda Brochettes on a Skewed Distribution
Uncle Ralph's Inverted Rice

Post Hoc

One-way Pavlova
Lemon Scheffé
Greco-Latin Squares
Least Squares (Dieter's delight)
Apple Phi & Cubed cheddar cheese

(Bartlett-Box lunch available)

Coffee and t-tests will be served in the Greenhouse–Geisser

Winer List

Hochtaler Eigenvalue 1979
Baron von Steiger 1964
Guttman Reisling 1978

(Newman–Keulade for the children)

Coretta Scott King will give an after dinner speech on "Degrees of Freedom"

Catered by James Frankish, Georgia Tiedemann,
M.A., Pat Manly, M.A., and Ken Reesor, M.A.
University of British Columbia

11
History and Systems of Psychology

Prescriptions for Fame in the History of Psychology

W. Scott Terry, Ph.D.
University of North Carolina at Charlotte

The present note describes a set of principles for becoming a famous psychologist. "Fame" in the present case does not simply mean literature citations, name recognition, or (these days) tenure. Rather, I am referring to a more enduring notoriety that will ensure one a place in future histories of psychology.

Most of us engage in various scholarly and professional endeavors, believing somehow these are traits of a good psychologist. As necessary as research and publication are to eventual success, these activities are not sufficient. After all, many are published but only a few are long remembered. This suggests some other qualities are also required. The difficulty is in determining what those qualities are that do lead an individual to be long remembered by succeeding generations. Possibly developing major theories, or new conceptualizations of the human psyche, are the keys to fame. But these are all rather nebulous and vague prescriptions, and may not be useful in guiding our everyday behavior.

What is needed is a set of behavioral guidelines, explicitly stating the requirements for historical fame. One source for these potential qualities is to look at our historical past for some hints. The present approach, using correlational and case study methods, is to look for common features in the professional lives of the early psychologists described in typical History and Systems texts. The assumption made is that there are certain attributes they possessed in common which set these individuals apart from others of their time, and which assured their eventual inclusion in the various histories of psychology.

Below are listed the prescriptions that became apparent after reading several standard history of psychology sources (e.g., R.I. Watson's *Great Psychologists,* the *History of Psychology in Autobiography* series, Hilgard's *American Psychology in Historical Perspective*). The psychologists described in these books obviously had what it takes to become famous, and thus should represent a valid source of information. The consistencies observed in the past may serve as guidelines for the future. Thus, if the reader were to conform their life to the following rules, then eventual and lasting fame can virtually be assured. The dozen factors uncovered so far are as follows:

1. *Be a graduate student under Wundt.* Many of Wundt's students went on to become well-known figures, including Kulpe, Krapelin, Titchener, Spearman, and Cattell. At least five early APA presidents were Wundt Ph.D.'s, and a few others did postdoctoral work under him.

2. *Don't be a Wundt student.* All of the psychologists described in History and Systems texts can be divided into two categories: those that were Wundt students, and those that were not.

3. *Read William James' Principles of Psychology.* The autobiographies of many great psychologists attest to their having read James as determining their choice of psychology as a career. Some early readers include Watson, Angel, Thorndike, Skinner, Hull, and even James himself. However, it is not clear whether the Principles contain valuable bits of information, or instead demonstrate the traits of stamina and perseverance.

4. *Have something named after you.* The "something" could be almost anything related to Psychology, but this rule will especially serve to keep your name on the tips-of-the-tongues of succeeding generations of students. Examples of the things to bear your namesake include: psychological effects (e.g., Zeigarnik and von Restorff); illusions (remember Müller-Lyer? Necker? Ponzo?); laws (such as the Weber-Fechner, Jost, or Yerkes-Dodson laws); a piece of laboratory apparatus (the famed Skinner box, Lashley III maze, or the Dodge pendulum photochronograph); a mental test (Rorschach, WISC); a statistical test (Spearman's rho or Pearson's r).

Finally, one might consider getting a building named after yourself (like William James Hall at Harvard). This may work even better than any of the others mentioned above. After all, isn't it more likely that someone will stumble over your name on a building, than on a book in the building?

5. *Be born during the years 1860–1880.* A simple count of birth years listed in one History and Systems text reveals an inverted-U shaped function, peaking during the years 1860–1880. Very few were born before 1800 and fewer still after 1940. If I were to pick a single year, it would probably have to be 1886 (Tolman, Guthrie, Koffka).

6. *Have a nervous breakdown.* Whether this should be properly labelled a mental breakdown (Galton), an existential crisis (James), or

a behavioral disorder (Watson) probably depends on your theoretical leanings.

7. *Be the First.* The first person to do something. Such as starting the first laboratory (Wundt or James); the first psychologist elected to the National Academy of Sciences (Pierce or Cattell); the first president of APA (G. Stanley Hall); the first president of a new University (Hall at Clark); the first American Ph.D. in psychology (Hall); found the first American journal of psychology (you guessed it, Hall).

8. *Don't be female.* While being male gives no assurance of success, few females have so far gotten their names into the textbooks. However, this handicap can be overcome by complying with some of the other prescriptions given here. For example, by having an effect named after oneself (Zeigarnik or von Restorff), or being the "first" at something (Mary Whiton Calkins was the first woman APA president, vhile Margaret Floy Washburn was Titchener's first Ph.D. student.)

9. *Get a degree from Harvard or Columbia* (before 1930) *or Yale* (anytime). (The latter reflects a personal bias.) These three schools have contributed 35 APA presidents. Although Harvard may lead the list in the number of famous graduates (e.g., James, Calkins, Angel, Holt, Tolman, Thorndike, and Yerkes were undergrad or graduate students there), one would expect such a diploma mill to turn out a few good people just by chance.

10. *First consider theology as a profession.* Several early psychologists attended theological schools (Hall and Ladd), and others report having contemplated the ministry before choosing psychology (Hull and Watson).

11. *Be an experimental psychologist.* If the past is any guide to the future, then the traditional areas of experimental psychology are *the* places to be. Apart from some discussion of psychoanalysis, most fields of clinical-personality-social psychology are underrepresented in the history texts. Granted, there are few jobs these days in experimental psychology. But this should only help reduce the competition for future success.

12. *Be the subject of a famous psychological study.* If you can't make it as a famous psychologist, why not try to be a famous subject? When a sample of graduating psych majors were asked to name three important historical figures, their answers were Freud, Skinner, and Little Albert. And who will ever forget the multiple personalities of Eve or Sybil? Footnotes in the texts now tell us that Freud's "Anna O" was really Bertha Pappenheim.

13. *Write papers on How To Become Famous.* I offer this as a tentative and undocumented prescription, that (hopefully) will be something of a self-fulfilling prophecy.

Deriving these initial principles is only a first step. Further research is needed to demonstrate more fully their validity. One test of these principles would be to find some past psychologists who actually satisfied several of these guidelines, and yet were not ever famous. Alternatively, one could set up a control condition of contemporary psychologists who are not destined to be remembered, and see if they fit any of the prescriptions mentioned above. This approach may involve some ethical questions, and I suspect few would want to volunteer for such a study. However, since the prescriptions listed above are based on a criterial group of distinguished psychologists, I would suggest the guidelines be accepted as working principles until more research is conducted.

12
Psychology Journals

Journel [sick] of Schizophrenic Processsssssss

Splitz Press Ink a magor farce in the field of PSYchology publishing is very very very happy fun to present a new journel --

the Journal [sick] of Schizophrenic Processsssssssssssssssssssssssssssssssss sssss

We anticipate their will be five (five) Issues for each of the seasons but they may TAKE one of them away from me.

I used to have three pens (pens), but my publisher stole them. He was jealous of my writing and she would often steal my ideas out of my head and replace them with Blocks of writer's block.

I called the CIA but they stole my pants and WANTED me to do something Terrrible. I refused to havee sex with the DOCTOR and he said

"I'll invade your parameters cogentinly"

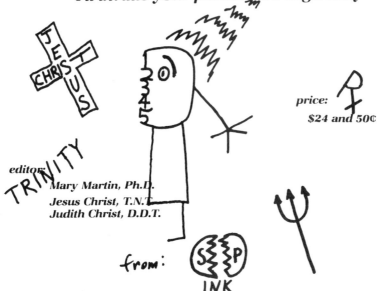

price:
$24 and 50¢

editor:
Mary Martin, Ph.D.
Jesus Christ, T.N.T.
Judith Christ, D.D.T.

from: INK

Ernst von Krankmann, Ph.D. and Ilene Bernstein

the journal of underachievement

vol. 1, no. 1   *spring 1985*

NEW! FOR 1985!

table of contents

Ernst von Krankmann, Ph.D. and Ilene Bernstein

13
Book Reviews

A Book Review—Buddha Meets Kohut: Western Civilization as a Transitional Object

Herbert R. Lochenkopf. Dukkha Press, 1983. 237 pages. $16.95 hardback.
Reviewed by Tom Greening, Ph.D.

Someone once asked Gandhi, "What do you think of Western Civilization?" Gandhi replied, "I think it would be a good idea." Lochenkopf, citing Winnicott, gives his qualified agreement that it is a "good-enough" idea, for the time being. He points out that before and since Gandhi we Westerners have been busy creating what for us passes as a civilization, Alan Watts, James Watt and the Watts Towers notwithstanding. But now our civilization faces the dual threat of nuclear holocaust and Lochenkopf's books. The threats are similar: Reading this book gave me the nausea of radiation sickness and made my hair fall out. One begins to suspect Lochenkopf is a mutant.

President Lowell of Harvard, introducing W. M. Wheeler for an honorary degree, remarked that Wheeler had shown that ants, like people, can build a complex society without recourse to reason. If ants eventually write books, they will probably resemble Lochenkopf's.

In this latest tome, Lochenkopf develops the theme he introduced in *Beyond Purpose and Meaning: Existence as Fraud* and perseverated on endlessly in *The Transmogrification: Beyond Transformation*. The implosive force of Lochenkopf's conceptual black holes could suck the meaning out of the *Encyclopedia Britannica*. Surely, characterizing Homo Novus sui generis as a borderline personality is going too far.

I did gain one insight from this book. I can finally understand the slogan of the orthodox, pre-object relations, Freudian psychologists: "If you meet the Kohut on the road, kill him."

A Book Review—Pathways to Consciousness: Hashish, Spinach Quiche, and Rajneesh

Herbert R. Lochenkopf. Dukkha Press, 1985. $11.95 hardback.
Reviewed by Tom Greening, Ph.D.

I owe an apology to Professor Lochenkopf. My negative review of his last book, *Buddha Meets Kohut: Western Civilization as a Transitional Object* [see *Journal of Polymorphous Perversity*, 1985, 2(1), 22], was merely my defensive response to his brilliant but unmerciful assault on the reality structures to which I have become inordinately attached. Letting go of them is painful, but having one's clutching fingers chopped off by Lochenkopf's razor-like mind is far worse. Professor Lochenkopf and I had a long discussion about my hostile review, and, with the help of his henchmen, I was finally able to perceive my errors. I can now heartily recommend *Buddha Meets Kohut* to anyone who seeks the Truth, in contrast to reality. I am grateful for this opportunity to review Lochenkopf's latest book and will try to be more objective.

Pathways to Consciousness: Hashish, Spinach Quiche, and Rajneesh is a penetrating essay about the evolution of middle class consciousness in the twentieth century. After an exhaustive analysis of the political and social impact of Karl Marx, Groucho Marx, and the Marx Toy Company, Lochenkopf concludes that Marxism, in all its forms, has failed and therefore succeeded as a liberation movement, due to its dreary and/or ludicrous materialism. Hashish and spinach quiche are the way out, says Lochenkopf, because eventually they cloy. "Liberation through Satiation" is his new anthem. Lochenkopf takes us on a Grand Tour of hip drug culture, the gourmet dining scene, and a sprawling real estate development in Oregon. In the process, he portrays the perilous pulchritude and pomposity of persnickety purveyors of pleasure. But he also traces the twisting, tortuous, titillating trail to triumphant transcendence.

While lauding Rajneesh for the delicate flavor of the spinach quiche served at the Oregon ashram, Lochenkopf inveighs against the guru for his anachronistic taste in cars, deriding the Rolls Royce as a monument to stodgy styling and engineering ennui. Its torque, 0–60 acceleration, power-to-weight ratio, and lateral g factor are paltry in comparison to Lochenkopf's own supercharged converted bread truck.

In conclusion, I highly recommend this book to anyone seeking higher consciousness, looking for a good quiche recipe, or tempted to buy a Rolls Royce.

14
Contemporary Issues in Psychology

Collaborative Research and Publication: An Experimental Investigation of the Dynamics Underlying the Trend Toward Multiple Authorship in Scholarly Psychological Publications[1]

Edward A. Polloway, Ed.D., Thomas A. Looney, Ph.D., G. Kenneth West, Ph.D., Renute N. Motroopin, Ph.D., J. David Smith, Ed.D., M.E. Gordon, Ed.D., Riccumulur Evita, Ph.D., Thomas W. Decker, Ph.D., Michael H. Epstein, Ed.D., Douglas Cullinan, Ed.D., James W. Patton, Ed.D., John T. McClure, M.A., Peter D. L. Warren, Ph.D., and Carl R. Smith, Ph.D.

Lynchburg College

An emerging trend in academic circles is the dramatic decline in individual research efforts as collaborative efforts become increasingly common. A recent report by Over (1982) illustrated this phenomenon by providing an analysis of this trend toward collaborative research and publication. He noted a distinct trend toward multiple authorship in the field of psychology, with the mean number of authors per publication increasing from 1.49 in 1949 to 2.19 in 1979. This trend was found to be consistent with publications in other disciplines within the natural and social sciences. Unfortunately, Over's analysis left unclear the precise reason(s) for the increase in professional collaboration and multiple authorship. Hence, the purpose of the present study was to identify the variable or variables responsible for the reported trend.

---

[1] The authors wish to acknowledge the assistance of B. Johnson for typing the manuscript, D. Elliott and J. Houston for assistance in copying the paper, H. Anstey and I. Burford for postal support, our respective college and university administrations for granting the requisite necessary leave time, and our spouses, families, and special friends for understanding our need to pursue this critical research. Data collection efforts were supported in part by the Theodore Roosevelt Foundation for Rugged Individualism.

Method

A total of 109 professional colleagues of the authors, teaching at a variety of distinguished institutions of higher learning throughout the United States, were asked to respond to the following questions:

1. Are you too dumb to produce scholarship on your own?
   Specify: Yes _____ No _____ Don't Know _____
2. Are you too unmotivated and/or uninspired to produce scholarship on your own?
   Specify: Yes _____ No _____ Don't Know _____
3. Are you unwilling to be held solely responsible for controversial opinions or for results that may not be replicable?
   Specify: Yes _____ No _____ Don't Know _____
4. Do you belong to a publication-of-the-month club,[2] which provides coauthorship on six or more publications in exchange for each publishable manuscript you individually claim to produce and supply the club?
   Specify: Yes _____ No _____ Don't Know _____

Results

A total of 14 individuals (coincidentally the number of authors of this paper) responded to the survey. Of these 14 respondents, 11 reported that they were too dumb to produce scholarship on their own, while 2 reported that they were not too dumb. One participant indicated "don't know," apparently due to an inability to understand the question in concert with generalized paranoia. Interestingly, two of the individuals who reported they were too dumb asked that their names be listed in the credits as anagrams.

Five subjects responded that they were not motivated or inspired (i.e., too lazy) to produce scholarship on their own, with the remaining nine responding "no" to this question, noting that rather they were simply too busy with grading papers, preparing lectures, interfacing or attending meaningless faculty meetings. All 14 subjects indicated an unwillingness to be held solely responsible for controversial opinions or results. Finally, while only five respondents reported that they

---

[2] If you would like to join such a club, send your membership fee of $500 in small unmarked bills to any of the authors (except the fifth author).

belonged to a publication-of-the-month club or similar organization, the remaining nine subjects did ask for membership information and included a set of self-addressed stamped envelopes (SASEs) with their responses.

Discussion

It is abundantly clear that the results contribute greatly to our understanding of the trend toward multiple authorship as reported by Over (1982), since these data provide a preliminary review of the significant reasons underlying this trend. Nevertheless, important issues remain. For example, five subjects reported belonging to a publication-of-the-month club and all others expressed interest in joining, yet a large majority believe they are too dumb to produce scholarship on their own. These data may seem in conflict, but this is true only if we assume that the manuscripts which individuals submit to such a club, and thus ultimately to professional journals, are in fact scholarly. This raises the question of the relationship between scholarship and publication in a host of academic disciplines. We do not know the answer at this time but do plan to address this question in subsequent study, which we will publish in the near future; potential collaborators should send their comments to the senior author.

Finally, although we feel that Over's (1982) analysis is legitimate, it is clearly too narrow in scope. We think that a similar analysis should be extended to other disciplines and to society in general. For example, recent research reported by Carlisle (1982) indicated an increasing trend toward collaborative prescription writing and filling among physicians and pharmacists, respectively. Also, consider how many of the Christmas cards you received last year were from more than one person. Is someone taking undue credit? Our pilot study (Looney & Polloway, in press) has suggested that this may be a trend; we anticipate having a more substantial data base on this question shortly after the holiday season.

References

Carlisle, K. (1982). Collaboration in pharmaceutical intervention: Fact or artifact. *Journal of Pharmacological Excesses, 32,* 147–183.

Looney, T.A., & Polloway, E.A. (in press). Collaboration at Christmas: Strategies to beat the holiday rush. *Hallmark Journal of Communication.*

Over, R. (1982). Collaborative research and publication in psychology. *American Psychologist, 37,* 996–1001.

Ethical Principles of Psychologists: An Update

Joel Herscovitch, Ph.D.

St. Joseph's Hospital
London, Ontario

The following list of ethical principles is offered as a way of updating the American Psychological Association's (1981) somewhat outdated guidelines on professional ethics.

Principle 1: It is unethical to inquire about whether you are in the will of a suicidal patient.

Principle 2: It is unethical to refer to impotent patients as "noodle city."

Principle 3: It is unethical to bill for two for obese patients.

Principle 4: It is unethical to use whoopee cushions on anxious patients.

Principle 5: It is unethical to interpret "splitting" to Siamese twins.

Principle 6: It is unethical to refer to ECT as a kind of break-dancing.

Principle 7: It is unethical to interpret missed sessions due to death as resistance.

Principle 8: It is unethical to do John Wayne impersonations during a patient's homosexual panic.

Principle 9: It is unethical to measure the lateness of compulsive patients in milliseconds.

Principle 10: It is unethical to try to raise your rates during the bargaining phase of terminal illness.

Principle 11: It is unethical to diagnose a patient as borderline just because they are having more fun than you.

References

American Psychological Association (1981). *Ethical standards of psychologists.* Washington, D.C.: APA.

A Grammatical Overview of Medical Records: The Write Stuff

Corey D. Fox, Ph.D.

The following quotes were lifted verbatim from the medical records of a general hospital in a large metropolitan area.

"Patient suffers from headaches while menstruating on the top of her head."

"There is a pressure bandage on the hip which is markedly swollen and tender."

"Patient is a newborn infant delivered over an intact perineum which cried spontaneously."

"Patient experiences difficulty swallowing tires easily."

"Patient had bronchoscopy today. Exam showed normal bowel to 25 cm."

"History: Patient was shot in head with .32 caliber rifle. Chief Complaint: Headache."

"Patient has difficulty walking on Digitalis."

"Patient had a D&C a year ago and all of her eyebrows came off."

"Patient referred to hospital for repair of hernia by a social service worker."

"Patient sent to hospital for erosion of the cervix by a local medical doctor."

Dictated: "Patient had a Pap smear today." Transcribed: "Patient had a Pabst Beer today."

"This was a nonsterile delivery by the nurse in the bed of a five pound male infant."

"Patient was struck by an auto while she was walking across the street at approximately 45 miles per hour."

"Patient complains of worsening acne and itching rash as well as nasal congestion of his trunk."

"Patient referred to hospital by private physician with green stools."

"This 54-year-old female is complaining of abdominal cramps with BM's on the one hand and constipation on the other."

"This mother of a 2-year-old desires a circumcision."

216

"Patient has been married twice, but denies any other serious illnesses."

"Patient's wife hit him over the head with an ironing board which now has six stitches on it."

"Patient is separated from his wife, and he also is allergic to Penicillin."

"This 8-year-old came to the GU clinic with his mother who has an absent right testicle since birth."

"Patient has no children and she doesn't smoke or drink either."

"She moves her bowels roughly, three times a day."

"This GU patient states he urinates around the clock every two hours."

[Male patient] "Pelvic exam: Deferred."

"Rx: Mycostatin vaginal suppositories, #24, Sig: Insert daily until exhausted."